**DO NOT REMOVE
CARDS FROM POCKET**

D0113131

Against Theory

Literary Studies and the New Pragmatism

Edited by W.J.T. Mitchell

The University of Chicago Press
Chicago and London

The articles in this volume originally appeared in the following issues of *Critical Inquiry:*
Summer 1982, Volume 8, no. 4; June 1983, Volume 9, no. 4; and March 1985, Volume
11, no. 3.

The University of Chicago Press, Chicago 60637
The University of Chicago Press, Ltd. London

Library of Congress Cataloging in Publication Data
Main entry under title:

Against theory.

　　Articles which originally appeared in Critical
inquiry from 1982 to 1985.
　　"These essays were written in response to the essay
Against theory, by Stephen Knapp and Walter Benn Michaels,
first published in Critical inquiry in summer of 1982"—
Introd.
　　Bibliography: p.
　　1. Criticism—Addresses, essays, lectures. 2. Litera-
ture—History and criticism—Theory, etc.—Addresses,
essays, lectures. 3. Knapp, Stephen. Against theory—
Addresses, essays, lectures. I. Mitchell, W. J. Thomas,
1942-
PN85.A35　　1985　　801'.95　　84-29127
ISBN 0-226-53226-7
ISBN 0-226-53227-5 (pbk.)

Contents

Introduction: Pragmatic Theory

The following collection of essays might as well be entitled *A Defense of Theory* as *Against Theory*. Most of the contributors defend some version of literary theory, either as a mode of critical practice or as a body of thought which stands outside critical practice and provides it with basic principles, methods, and investigative problems. The reason for the potentially misleading title is that all these essays were written in response to Steven Knapp and Walter Benn Michaels' essay "Against Theory," first published in *Critical Inquiry* in summer 1982. Seven responses, as well as Knapp and Michaels' rejoinder, appeared in the June 1983 issue of *Critical Inquiry*, and are all reprinted here, along with two new statements by Richard Rorty and Stanley Fish and a final reply by Knapp and Michaels. The controversy has drawn so much attention among literary critics that it seemed appropriate to collect it in a single volume where the course of the debate can be followed from start to finish.

As in most debates, part of the controversy is over the question of just what is at issue. What is theory, in the study of literature or in other disciplines? What is at stake in being "for" or "against" theory? What sorts of values and interests are being challenged (and endorsed) by the antitheoretical arguments of those who are sometimes called the "New Pragmatists" (Fish, Knapp, Michaels, and Rorty) in literary study? One thing that will quickly become apparent to the reader of this collection is that the sides in this debate do not settle into two clearly defined camps. Those who defend theory against Knapp and Michaels do so for all sorts of different reasons, and they represent a wide range of theoretical positions, from the interpretive realism and historicism of E. D. Hirsch, Jr., to the textual objectivism of Hershel Parker, to the deconstructionist orientation of Jonathan Crewe. The pragmatic, antitheoretical camp is not completely unified either: Knapp and Michaels chide Fish for occasional lapses into the theoretical mode, and Rorty finds himself at odds with a movement that, some would say, he largely helped to create with his efforts to revive the American pragmatist tradition and ally it with certain antitheoretical tendencies in European philosophy.

What is the importance of all this fuss over theory in literary studies? A gross oversimplification of the controversy might go this way: in the last twenty years, theory has, for a variety of reasons, become one of the "glamour" fields in academic literary study. Structuralism, semiotics, hermeneutics, deconstruction, speech-act theory, reception theory, psychoanalytic theory, feminism, Marxism, and various philosophical "approaches" have become a familiar part of the professional structure of literary study. Any literature department that does not have a "theorist" of some sort on its faculty is clearly out of step. More important, any specialist trained in one of the traditional historical fields in literary history is likely to be asked what sort of theory he or she subscribes to. The general assumption is that everyone has a theory that governs his or her practice, and the only issue is whether one is self-conscious about that theory. Not to be aware of one's theoretical assumptions is to be a mere practitioner, slogging along in the routines of scholarship and interpretation.

Given the dominance of theory in contemporary literary study, it was inevitable that someone would issue a challenge to it. We might say, in fact, that the antitheoretical polemic is one of the characteristic genres of theoretical discourse: the philosophy of science has Paul Feyerabend's *Against Method;* Marxist criticism has E. P. Thompson's *Poverty of Theory.* And one of the most influential branches of modern theory in literature and philosophy is called "antifoundationalism," a thoroughgoing skepticism that calls into question all claims to ground discourse in fundamental principles, "facts," or logical procedures. From a very broad perspective, then, "Against Theory" may be seen as an inevitable dialectical moment within theoretical discourse, the moment when theory's constructive, positive tendency generates its own negation. From a narrower professional perspective, it should be clear why Knapp and Michaels' antitheoretical arguments, whatever their particular merits, strike many critics as scandalous. The challenge is not just to a way of thinking and writing but to a way of making a living. If Knapp and Michaels are right, then it looks as though a whole generation of scholars is out of work: "If accepted, our arguments would indeed eliminate the 'career option' of writing and teaching theory" (p. 105).

Not surprisingly, then, most of those who respond to "Against Theory" think Knapp and Michaels are wrong. Some (like Crewe and Daniel O'Hara) define their "error" in political and moral terms, characterizing the "New Pragmatism" as a "petty theodicy of the guild," a cynical nihilism that "comforts the champions of the status quo" (pp. 60, 37). Others (the majority) are more dispassionate. They find various particular problems in "Against Theory" that are more or less damaging to its argument, while acknowledging that the essay raises important questions. All would agree, I think, that "Against Theory" is a tour de force, whether for good or ill: it is absolutely sure of its position, rarely hedging or qualifying its attack on literary theory; it is disconcertingly ingenious in its rhetorical and argumentative strategies, an ingenuity that continues unabated in Knapp and Michaels' replies to their critics; it is undeniably witty in its mustering of examples (Crewe notes, somewhat ruefully, that the example of the wave-poem is "destined no doubt to become famous" [p. 60]). Probably the most fascinating feature of the essay is its spare, laconic, almost enigmatic style. The crisp declarative sentences of "Against Theory" contain none of the notorious jargon of literary theory; no special expertise is needed to read it. But the clarity of Knapp and Michaels' argument against theory is accompanied by a studious reserve about motives. The essay gives the impression that its authors are in the grip of an insight that is quite indifferent to questions of value, interest, or power. They declare insouciantly that their argument has "no consequences" and that it is "indifferent" to the existence of professional literary study (p. 105). It is hardly surprising that these tacit denials of political or self- interest have provoked charges that the essay is a sort of careerist exercise which promotes a reactionary politics. Perhaps the most paradoxical and intriguing feature of "Against Theory" is that an essay which argues that meaning and intention are essentially the same thing should be so clear about its meaning while remaining so inscrutable about its intentions.

The essential value of "Against Theory," then, aside from its merits as a piece of writing in itself, is its function as a catalyst, a provocation to dialogue. Even if Knapp and Michaels are wrong both in their general claims about the function of theory and in their specific argument about meaning and intention, their "error" has the sort of clarity and definition that encourages the articulation of unsuspected insights. "Against Theory" has provided an ideal test case for *Critical Inquiry*'s central editorial principle, the notion of what I have elsewhere called "dialectical pluralism."[1] This principle suggests that certain kinds of "errors," ably and vigorously de-fended, are far more interesting than a host of truths universally ac-knowledged and (for that reason) left unexamined. Knapp and Michaels help us to see theory's need to defend, not merely assume, its value for critical practice, and they provide the occasion for this defense on a very broad front, one that does not (in the usual fashion) pit one theory against another but asks us to see the project of literary theory as a coherent whole, united by certain fundamental problems of common concern.

All the defenses of theory in this collection of essays would have to be called "pragmatic." O'Hara and Crewe suggest that theory is a goad to critical progress and reform, providing models for practice and for the evaluation of practice. Steven Mailloux proposes that theory be regarded as a distinct kind of rhetorical practice, one that has had far-reaching consequences for other modes of critical practice. Adena Rosmarin and Rorty see literary theory as a place for a fruitful conversation between literature and philosophy. Hirsch, Parker, and William Dowling use "Against Theory" as an occasion to clarify specific problems in the notion

1. W. J. T. Mitchell, *"Critical Inquiry* and the Ideology of Pluralism," *Critical Inquiry* 8 (Summer 1982): 613.

4   W. J. T. Mitchell

of textual meaning, particularly the relation between "authorial" meaning
and "textual" or "formal" conditions of meaning—the choice between
grounding a text's meaning in "its" author or "an" author.

None of these defenses, it should be noted, take up the challenge
to defend theory in what Fish calls the "strong" sense, the "dream of
Baconian method" which would (in the manner of Noam Chomsky's
linguistics), provide a "general hermeneutics," a model of "a general
rationality" that would be "independent" of "contingencies," "contextual
circumstances," and "interested judgments" (pp. 120, 110, 111, 110).
Perhaps it is simply too late in the day for such a defense: since Wittgenstein,
or perhaps since Stanley Cavell's reading of Wittgenstein, the temptation
to refute skepticism (and reinstate the strongest claims of philosophical
reason) has seemed less and less attractive. The main devotees of strong,
nontrivial theory these days are its skeptical opponents, who require the
presence of a priggish, authoritarian positivist in order to have something
to oppose. This may explain why the closest we come in these pages to
a theory in the strong, old-fashioned sense is in the writing of Knapp
and Michaels. As they say in their first reply to their critics: "Our account
of interpretation, if true, describes the way interpretation *always* works,
irrespective of its relation to any institution" (p. 105). If this sounds
suspiciously like Fish's description of a "general hermeneutics" that would
be free of "interested judgments," the resemblance becomes even more
striking when Knapp and Michaels address directly the question of interests
and motives:

> Nothing in "Against Theory" tells you whether programs in women's
> studies are a good thing, whether teachers should be tenured, or
> whether graduate programs should be maintained or cut back in
> response to the current job crisis. This is not to deny that we ourselves
> have views on these questions, just as we have views on the relative
> merits of historical scholarship and close reading; it is only to insist
> that such views have no relation to our account of interpretation.
> [P. 105]

The only difference between Knapp and Michaels and the strong theorists
they oppose is their renunciation of power, their recurrent claim that
their account of interpretation has no consequences for practice (since it
just describes what we always must do) and only one consequence for
theory: "Theory should stop" (p. 105).

One could reply, of course, that theory in the strong sense has
already stopped. When it does rear its head (as in Chomsky's linguistics),
its strongest claims are generally regarded as a form of what Fish calls
"theory hope," the temporary euphoria that often accompanies an intellectual breakthrough. The countertradition of "theory fear" (skepticism
and antifoundationalism) seems strong enough, however, to prevent our

being taken in by false hopes (p. 112). Since the skeptical tradition seems to dominate current literary theory, the challenge at the present time would seem to be a defense of theory hope. Knapp and Michaels set the stage for such a defense in two ways, one highly general, the other quite specific. The general result of their argument is to provoke a pragmatic and historically self-conscious understanding of theory. Their more specific contribution is to a "special project"—the theory of literary meaning—which has dominated literary criticism at least since the New Critics (p. 11).

Knapp and Michaels stake out a position on the problem of intention that, while it may strike some as counterintuitive or philosophically naive, has something like the tonic effect that W. K. Wimsatt and Monroe Beardsley's classic essay "The Intentional Fallacy" had on a generation of critics.[2] Wimsatt and Beardsley argued that the only intention worthy of critical interest would be one that was fully realized in the text; the need to discuss any other intention, to ask the author what he or she really meant, for instance, would simply be evidence of artistic failure. Knapp and Michaels, by contrast, seem quite indifferent to the question of where the intention is discovered (in "the work itself," in ancillary documents, or in the author's testimony). Their only claim is that interpretation, the finding of meaning, just *is* the finding of intention. To look for one is to look for the other, because they are just the same thing. The fall into theory occurs when we begin to think that meaning and intention are something different and devise a method for finding one by looking for the other. Historicists like Hirsch think that we find meaning by ascertaining intention; formalists like Wimsatt and Beardsley (and, more recently, Paul de Man) think that meaning will take care of itself if we "subtract" extrinsic intention and let the language of the text work on us.

What, aside from the startling rhetorical effect of outflanking all the major theories of literary intention, does this conflation of meaning and intention accomplish? It certainly will not accomplish what Wimsatt and Beardsley did: it will not produce a school of followers who will set about discovering the perfect embodiment of meaning in the formal qualities of texts. "Against Theory" deliberately renounces any such ambitions to redirect the activity of practical criticism. But it just might (as it has already, in this volume) produce a loosely defined "school" of antagonists who will take up the challenge to formulate a pragmatic account of theory, one that would identify theory as a genre of writing, a type of discourse.

This view of theory might take up Mailloux's suggestion that theory be understood rhetorically. Such a view would redescribe the opposition

2. See W. K. Wimsatt and Monroe C. Beardsley, "The Intentional Fallacy," *The Verbal Icon: Studies in the Meaning of Poetry* (Lexington, Ky., 1954), pp. 3–18.

between theory and practice as a system of figurative contrasts and not as a metaphysical divide that situates theory (in Fish's strong sense) beyond contingency. The outlines of this rhetorical account of theory might take the following form:

THEORY IS	THEORY IS NOT
reflection	immediate perception
fundamental principles	surface phenomena
models, schemes, systems	things in themselves
large-scale guesswork	small-scale certainty
metaphysics	physics
speculation	traditional wisdom
intuition	discursive reasoning
abstract thought	concrete experience
deductive or inductive	adductive[3]
a priori, a posteriori	in between

These two columns of terms display some of the contrasts we make between the theoretical and the nontheoretical *in practice*. Some of them take the form of antitheses (abstract/concrete, guess/certainty) that involve associated figurative contrasts (large/small, high/low, depth/surface, container/contained, representation/represented). Of particular interest is the connection between theory and its Greek roots in visual terminology. Theory, according to the *Oxford English Dictionary*, is "a looking at, viewing, contemplation, speculation; also a sight, spectacle." There is a tacit contrast here between the visual as the "noblest" sense and the lower, more practical senses, particularly hearing, the conduit of the oral tradition, of stories rather than systems, sententiae rather than schematisms. Theory

3. In correspondence about this essay, Richard Rorty questioned my use of the term "adductive" (as contrasted with "deductive" and "inductive") to characterize what "theory is not" in contrast to what "theory is." What I had in mind was the practice of citation and exemplification, the "adducing" of precedents as a ground or justification for a present judgment. Adduction may proceed with reference to a general principle, perhaps even a full-blown theory, but it seems to me that what Nelson Goodman would call the "route" of this sort of reference is different from that of deduction and induction. Deduction proceeds from generals to particulars; induction, from particulars to generals; and adduction, from particulars to particulars. These particulars may illustrate or exemplify general principles, but the process of adduction itself always remains at the level of concrete particulars. If I want to show that a rule applies in this particular case, I cite a previous case where it applied, or I adduce some hypothetical example. A lawyer adduces precedents (which are always particular cases and judgments) or evidence in support of the application of the law to a present case; a literary critic, similarly, adduces a set of canonical examples to identify the tradition, genre, or convention that fits some text that has not yet been "placed" in the literary universe. There's no question that theory and general principles function throughout adductive procedures, but they stand, as it were, off to the side of the process, taken for granted, not themselves in question. Adduction doesn't ask, What is pastoral? but, rather, Is this a pastoral? Adductive proofs rely, therefore, quite heavily on authority and tradition.

is (*pace* Jacques Derrida) ocular, spatial, and graphocentric. Carl Hempel: Theory "may be likened to a complex spatial network [which] floats, as it were, above the plane of observation and is anchored to it by rules of interpretation."[4] Wittgenstein: "A model . . . is always part of the *symbolism* of a theory. Its advantage may be that it can be taken in at a glance and easily held in the mind. It has been said that a model, in a sense, dresses up the pure theory; that the *naked* theory is sentences or equations."[5]

Theory thus repeats within itself the oppositions that distinguish it from nontheory: naked/clothed, pure/applied, image/text. It is a composite form of discourse, partly observation, partly imagination. Arthur Danto: "Theory may be regarded as a system of laws, some of which are empirical."[6] Theory is monotheistic, in love with simplicity, scope, and coherence. It aspires to explain the many in terms of the one, and the greater the gap between the unitary simplicity of theory and the infinite multiplicity of things in its domain, the more powerful the theory. Theory is thus to thought what power is to politics. Marx: Theory comprises "the ruling ideas" of an epoch—that is, "the ideas of the ruling class"—that is, "ideology."[7] But theory is also the critique of ideology, the expression of intellectual alienation, self-criticism, and reflection on the origins of theory. Theory always places itself at the beginning or the end of thought, providing first principles from which hypotheses, laws, and methods may be deduced, or summarizing, encoding, and schematizing practice in a general account. It is unhappy with the middle realm of history, practical conduct, and business as usual and so tends to seek a final solution, a utopian perspective, which presents itself as a point of origin.

The narrower task of a pragmatic theory of literature would, one assumes, take up the challenge presented by Knapp and Michaels' account of meaning. This inquiry might begin by asking, What happens if we apply Knapp and Michaels' equation of meaning and intention to their own *use* of the words "meaning" and "intention"? What happens to this claim if we (whether theorists or plain practitioners) *intend* these terms to mean something different? Are we simply mistaken, victims of a theoretical delusion that these two different words have two different meanings? If so, then the meaning of these words is not what we intend, and they violate Knapp and Michaels' general rule that intention and meaning are just the same thing. If we are not mistaken, on the other hand, then "intention" and "meaning" (like all other words) mean what we intend them to mean, which in this case involves their meaning something

4. Carl Hempel, quoted in *Encyclopedia of Philosophy*, rpt. ed., s.v. "Problems of Philosophy of Science," by Arthur C. Danto.

5. Ludwig Wittgenstein, *The Blue and Brown Books* (New York, 1958), p. 6.

6. *Encyclopedia of Philosophy*, s.v. "Problems of Philosophy of Science," by Danto.

7. Karl Marx, *The German Ideology, Part One*, ed. C. J. Arthur (New York, 1981), p. 64.

8   W. J. T. Mitchell

different from one another. For Knapp and Michaels to be right about
the meaning of words in general, they must make an exception (their
Archimedean fulcrum) for the words "meaning" and "intention." These
words alone mean not what we intend by them but something given by
their nature, which makes them synonymous despite our strongest desires
to intend something different by them.

Paradoxes like this are cheap, of course, and I bring this one up not
to discredit Knapp and Michaels' claim but to clarify its status. The notion
that meaning and intention are just the same thing is, in one sense,
intuitively obvious, and Knapp and Michaels don't really need to make
an argument for it. They can simply begin (as they do) by stipulating it
("once it is seen that . . . meaning . . . is simply identical to . . . intended
meaning . . ." [p. 12]). One suspects that they *could* argue for such a
stipulation and that an impressive list of philosophers of language (John
Searle, Donald Davidson, and Charles Sanders Peirce come up in their
footnotes) could be mustered on their side of the question. One might
then muster another group of philosophers on the other side to argue
that meaning and intention are not identical, a list that would probably
include Gottlob Frege and Wittgenstein, among others. This confrontation
would quickly leave the literary theorists out in the cold, bewailing their
inability to judge who has the better arguments and finally attaching
themselves to the camp that seemed most congenial to what they were
already inclined to do.

My point in this scenario is that the central thesis of "Against Theory"
is no more or less "theoretical," no more or less "pragmatic" or intuitive,
than its antithesis. Say we have an intuition, equally strong, that meaning
and intention are not the same thing. The question is, What is the relation
between these two intuitions? And what happens when they are elaborated
into theories and methods? Consider, first, some practical instances, provided by Cavell, of the difference between meaning and intention:

> If I glance at you meaningfully, that is between us, but if I glance
> at you intentionally, I am including a third. I may give up a pawn
> unintentionally in poorly carrying out a strategy, but if I give it up
> meaninglessly, the strategy itself was poor. I know how to give the
> meaning of a word but not how to give the intention of a word,
> though I might tell you what someone intended in using a certain
> word in a certain place. If Hamlet had asked, "Do you think I
> intended country matters?" Ophelia might well have been even
> more alarmed than she was.[8]

If Knapp and Michaels want to rescue us from the illegitimate sovereignty
of theory and restore us to the freedom of ungrounded practice, they
will find that practice is riddled with the very same distinctions they found

8. Stanley Cavell, "The Division of Talent," *Critical Inquiry* 11 (forthcoming, June 1985).

objectionable in theory. Perhaps these distinctions will not have the same coercive force they have in the realm of theory; perhaps they will not make the same claims to produce foolproof methods for ascertaining meaning. But the point is that there is no escaping these distinctions in the realm of practice. The "fall into division," as William Blake would put it, has always already occurred.

Knapp and Michaels do seem right, however, in suggesting that these divisions, regardless of their origins in practice, do provide the fundamental machinery for theory. Again, Cavell shows how this move from practical usage to theory might go:

> Here compare: if the woman who dropped the slipper is the same as the woman who ran from the ball, you can say truly that looking for the one (the one the slipper fits) just *is* looking for the other (the runaway love). But is it (therefore) *hard* to see how looking for one provides an objective method for looking for the other? It seems, on the contrary, that in this case it is *because* the woman in question is the same under two (or three) different descriptions that a method for looking is established.[9]

The same point might be made with scientific method, where descriptions of a shiny yellow metal and a mineral with a certain specific gravity might refer to the same thing but suggest, by virtue of their difference, a definite procedure for finding gold.

Knapp and Michaels seem right, then, in pointing to these sorts of differentiations, the desynonymizing of terms that have the same reference, as one of the fundamental characteristics of theoretical discourse. Where they seem wrong is in their claim that these distinctions originate in theory and that their abolition would lead to the collapse of theory and a return to practice. Actually, the distinctions arise in practice, in ordinary usage, and are developed into theories that (like all theories) are doomed to "fail" at one point or another—"fail" in the sense of not achieving the goal of complete mastery that Fish attributes to theory in the strong, nontrivial sense.

By a curious route, then, Knapp and Michaels out-theorize the theorists. Only in theory would anyone want to deny that there is a difference between meaning and intention; in practice, we use the distinction all the time. Only in theory would we want (as Knapp and Michaels do) to collapse the distinction between "knowledge" and "true belief" (in practice, to say that I *believe* something to be the case is tantamount to saying that I do not *know* it for a fact). The only question is, as Rosmarin suggests, What sort of theory would want to suspend these distinctions—and what other sorts of commonsense distinctions does it retain as foundational assumptions? Where would such a theory lead us? The answer of Michaels,

9. Ibid.

Knapp, and Fish is unequivocal: it leads nowhere. This is a theory that has no consequences in the sense that theories have always wanted to have consequences—that is, by suggesting methods, pedagogical routines, procedures of verification, and so forth. If we take them literally (or, should I say, if the authors mean what they say), this is a theory of pure self-negation, what O'Hara calls "revisionary madness," articulating what many will see as the ultimate nihilism of contemporary theory. But if it is nihilism, it is one that demands an answer, not easy polemical dismissal— one that calls for theory to clarify its claims, not to mystify them with the easy assurance of intellectual fashion and institutional authority. If this volume aids in that clarification, it will have served its purpose.

W. J. T. Mitchell

Against Theory

Steven Knapp and Walter Benn Michaels

1

By "theory" we mean a special project in literary criticism: the attempt to govern interpretations of particular texts by appealing to an account of interpretation in general. The term is sometimes applied to literary subjects with no direct bearing on the interpretation of individual works, such as narratology, stylistics, and prosody. Despite their generality, however, these subjects seem to us essentially empirical, and our argument against theory will not apply to them.

Contemporary theory has taken two forms. Some theorists have sought to ground the reading of literary texts in methods designed to guarantee the objectivity and validity of interpretations. Others, impressed by the inability of such procedures to produce agreement among interpreters, have translated that failure into an alternative mode of theory that denies the possibility of correct interpretation. Our aim here is not to choose between these two alternatives but rather to show that both rest on a single mistake, a mistake that is central to the notion of theory per se. The object of our critique is not a particular way of doing theory but the idea of doing theory at all.

Theory attempts to solve—or to celebrate the impossibility of solving—a set of familiar problems: the function of authorial intention, the status of literary language, the role of interpretive assumptions, and so on. We will not attempt to solve these problems, nor will we be con-

Reprinted from the Summer 1982 issue of *Critical Inquiry*.

cerned with tracing their history or surveying the range of arguments they have stimulated. In our view, the mistake on which all critical theory rests has been to imagine that these problems are real. In fact, we will claim such problems only seem real—and theory itself only seems possible or relevant—when theorists fail to recognize the fundamental inseparability of the elements involved.

The clearest example of the tendency to generate theoretical problems by splitting apart terms that are in fact inseparable is the persistent debate over the relation between authorial intention and the meaning of texts. Some theorists have claimed that valid interpretations can only be obtained through an appeal to authorial intentions. This assumption is shared by theorists who, denying the possibility of recovering authorial intentions, also deny the possibility of valid interpretations. But once it is seen that the meaning of a text is simply identical to the author's intended meaning, the project of *grounding* meaning in intention becomes incoherent. Since the project itself is incoherent, it can neither succeed nor fail; hence both theoretical attitudes toward intention are irrelevant. The mistake made by theorists has been to imagine the possibility or desirability of moving from one term (the author's intended meaning) to a second term (the text's meaning), when actually the two terms are the same. One can neither succeed nor fail in deriving one term from the other, since to have one is already to have them both.

In the following two sections we will try to show in detail how theoretical accounts of intention always go wrong. In the fourth section we will undertake a similar analysis of an influential account of the role interpretive assumptions or beliefs play in the practice of literary criticism. The issues of belief and intention are, we think, central to the theoretical enterprise; our discussion of them is thus directed not only against specific theoretical arguments but against theory in general. Our examples are meant to represent the central mechanism of all theoretical arguments, and our treatment of them is meant to indicate that all such arguments will fail and fail in the same way. If we are right, then the whole enterprise of critical theory is misguided and should be abandoned.

Steven Knapp, an assistant professor of English at the University of California, Berkeley, is currently working on a book about personification in eighteenth-century and Romantic literature. **Walter Benn Michaels,** an associate professor of English at the University of California, Berkeley, is working on the relation between literary and economic forms of representation in nineteenth-century America.

2. Meaning and Intention

The fact that what a text means is what its author intends is clearly stated by E. D. Hirsch when he writes that the meaning of a text "is, and can be, nothing other than the author's meaning" and "is determined once and for all by the character of the speaker's intention."[1] Having defined meaning as the author's intended meaning, Hirsch goes on to argue that all literary interpretation "must stress a reconstruction of the author's aims and attitudes in order to evolve guides and norms for construing the meaning of his text." Although these guides and norms cannot guarantee the correctness of any particular reading—nothing can—they nevertheless constitute, he claims, a "fundamentally sound" and "objective" method of interpretation (pp. 224, 240).

What seems odd about Hirsch's formulation is the transition from definition to method. He begins by defining textual meaning as the author's intended meaning and then suggests that the best way to find textual meaning is to look for authorial intention. But if meaning and intended meaning are already the same, it's hard to see how looking for one provides an objective method—or any sort of method—for looking for the other; looking for one just *is* looking for the other. The recognition that what a text means and what its author intends it to mean are identical should entail the further recognition that any appeal from one to the other is useless. And yet, as we have already begun to see, Hirsch thinks the opposite; he believes that identifying meaning with the expression of intention has the supreme theoretical usefulness of providing an objective method of choosing among alternative interpretations.

Hirsch, however, has failed to understand the force of his own formulation. In one moment he identifies meaning and intended meaning; in the next moment he splits them apart. This mistake is clearly visible in his polemic against formalist critics who deny the importance of intention altogether. His argument against these critics ends up invoking their account of meaning at the expense of his own. Formalists, in Hirsch's summary, conceive the text as a " 'piece of language,' " a "public object whose character is defined by public norms." The problem with this account, according to Hirsch, is that "no mere sequence of words can represent an actual verbal meaning with reference to public norms alone. Referred to these alone, the text's meaning remains indeterminate." Hirsch's example, "My car ran out of gas," is, as he notes, susceptible to an indeterminate range of interpretations. There

1. E. D. Hirsch, Jr., *Validity in Interpretation* (New Haven, Conn., 1967), pp. 216, 219. Our remarks on Hirsch are in some ways parallel to criticisms offered by P. D. Juhl in the second chapter of his *Interpretation: An Essay in the Philosophy of Literary Criticism* (Princeton, N.J., 1980). Juhl's position will be discussed in the next section. All further citations to these works will be included in the text.

are no public norms which will help us decide whether the sentence means that my automobile lacks fuel or "my Pullman dash[ed] from a cloud of Argon." Only by assigning a particular intention to the words "My car ran out of gas" does one arrive at a determinate interpretation. Or, as Hirsch himself puts it, "The array of possibilities only begins to become a more selective system of *probabilities* when, instead of confronting merely a word sequence, we also posit a speaker who very likely means something" (p. 225).[2]

This argument seems consistent with Hirsch's equation of meaning and intended meaning, until one realizes that Hirsch is imagining a moment of interpretation before intention is present. This is the moment at which the text's meaning "remains indeterminate," before such indeterminacy is cleared up by the *addition* of authorial intention. But if meaning and intention really are inseparable, then it makes no sense to think of intention as an ingredient that needs to be added; it must be present from the start. The issue of determinacy or indeterminacy is irrelevant. Hirsch thinks it's relevant because he thinks, correctly, that the movement from indeterminacy to determinacy involves the addition of information, but he also thinks, incorrectly, that adding information amounts to adding intention. Since intention is already present, the only thing added, in the movement from indeterminacy to determinacy, is information *about* the intention, not the intention itself. For a sentence like "My car ran out of gas" even to be recognizable as a sentence, we must already have posited a speaker and hence an intention. Pinning down an interpretation of the sentence will not involve adding a speaker but deciding among a range of possible speakers. Knowing that the speaker inhabits a planet with an atmosphere of inert gases and on which the primary means of transportation is railroad will give one interpretation; knowing that the speaker is an earthling who owns a Ford will give another. But even if we have none of this information, as soon as we attempt to interpret at all we are already committed to a characterization of the speaker as a speaker of language. We know, in other words, that the speaker intends to speak; otherwise we wouldn't be interpreting. In this latter case, we have less information about the speaker than in the other two (where we at least knew the speaker's planetary origin), but the relative lack of information has nothing to do with the presence or absence of intention.

This mistake no doubt accounts for Hirsch's peculiar habit of calling the proper object of interpretation the "author's meaning" and, in later writings, distinguishing between it and the "reader's meaning."[3] The choice between these two kinds of meaning becomes, for Hirsch, an ethical imperative as well as an "operational" necessity. But if all mean-

2. The phrase "piece of language" goes back, Hirsch notes, to the opening paragraph of William Empson's *Seven Types of Ambiguity*, 3d ed. (New York, 1955).
3. See Hirsch, *The Aims of Interpretation* (Chicago, 1976), p. 8.

ing is always the author's meaning, then the alternative is an empty one, and there is no choice, ethical or operational, to be made. Since theory is designed to help us make such choices, all theoretical arguments on the issue of authorial intention must at some point accept the premises of anti-intentionalist accounts of meaning. In debates about intention, the moment of imagining intentionless meaning constitutes the theoretical moment itself. From the standpoint of an argument against critical theory, then, the only important question about intention is whether there can in fact be intentionless meanings. If our argument against theory is to succeed, the answer to this question must be no.

The claim that all meanings are intentional is not, of course, an unfamiliar one in contemporary philosophy of language. John Searle, for example, asserts that "there is no getting away from intentionality," and he and others have advanced arguments to support this claim.[4] Our purpose here is not to add another such argument but to show how radically counterintuitive the alternative would be. We can begin to get a sense of this simply by noticing how difficult it is to imagine a case of intentionless meaning.

Suppose that you're walking along a beach and you come upon a curious sequence of squiggles in the sand. You step back a few paces and notice that they spell out the following words:

> A slumber did my spirit seal;
> I had no human fears:
> She seemed a thing that could not feel
> The touch of earthly years.[5]

This would seem to be a good case of intentionless meaning: you recognize the writing as writing, you understand what the words mean, you may even identify them as constituting a rhymed poetic stanza—and all this without knowing anything about the author and indeed without needing to connect the words to any notion of an author at all. You can do all these things without thinking of anyone's intention. But now suppose that, as you stand gazing at this pattern in the sand, a wave washes up and recedes, leaving in its wake (written below what you now realize was only the first stanza) the following words:

> No motion has she now, no force;
> She neither hears nor sees;
> Rolled round in earth's diurnal course,
> With rocks, and stones, and trees.

---

4. John R. Searle, "Reiterating the Differences: A Reply to Derrida," *Glyph* 1 (1977): 202.
5. Wordsworth's lyric has been a standard example in theoretical arguments since its adoption by Hirsch; see *Validity in Interpretation*, pp. 227–30 and 238–40.

One might ask whether the question of intention still seems as irrelevant as it did seconds before. You will now, we suspect, feel compelled to explain what you have just seen. Are these marks mere accidents, produced by the mechanical operation of the waves on the sand (through some subtle and unprecedented process of erosion, percolation, etc.)? Or is the sea alive and striving to express its pantheistic faith? Or has Wordsworth, since his death, become a sort of genius of the shore who inhabits the waves and periodically inscribes on the sand his elegiac sentiments? You might go on extending the list of explanations indefinitely, but you would find, we think, that all the explanations fall into two categories. You will either be ascribing these marks to some agent capable of intentions (the living sea, the haunting Wordsworth, etc.), or you will count them as nonintentional effects of mechanical processes (erosion, percolation, etc.). But in the second case—where the marks now seem to be accidents—will they still seem to be words?

Clearly not. They will merely seem to *resemble* words. You will be amazed, perhaps, that such an astonishing coincidence could occur. Of course, you would have been no less amazed had you decided that the sea or the ghost of Wordsworth was responsible. But it's essential to recognize that in the two cases your amazement would have two entirely different sources. In one case, you would be amazed by the identity of the author—who would have thought that the sea can write poetry? In the other case, however, in which you accept the hypothesis of natural accident, you're amazed to discover that what you thought was poetry turns out not to be poetry at all. It isn't poetry because it isn't language; that's what it means to call it an accident. As long as you thought the marks were poetry, you were assuming their intentional character. You had no idea who the author was, and this may have tricked you into thinking that positing an author was irrelevant to your ability to read the stanza. But in fact you had, without realizing it, already posited an author. It was only with the mysterious arrival of the second stanza that your tacit assumption (e.g., someone writing with a stick) was challenged and you realized that you had made one. Only now, when positing an author seems impossible, do you genuinely imagine the marks as authorless. But to deprive them of an author is to convert them into accidental likenesses of language. They are not, after all, an example of intentionless meaning; as soon as they become intentionless they become meaningless as well.

The arrival of the second stanza made clear that what had seemed to be an example of intentionless language was either not intentionless or not language. The question was whether the marks counted as language; what determined the answer was a decision as to whether or not they were the product of an intentional agent. If our example has seemed farfetched, it is only because there is seldom occasion in our culture to wonder whether the *sea* is an intentional agent. But there *are* cases where the question of intentional agency might be an important and difficult one. Can computers speak? Arguments over this question reproduce exactly the terms of our example. Since computers are machines, the issue of whether they can speak seems to hinge on the possibility of intentionless language. But our example shows that there is no such thing as intentionless language; the only real issue is whether computers are capable of intentions. However this issue may be decided—and our example offers no help in deciding it—the decision will not rest on a theory of meaning but on a judgment as to whether computers can be intentional agents. This is not to deny that a great deal—morally, legally, and politically—might depend on such judgments. But no degree of practical importance will give these judgments theoretical force.

The difference between theoretical principle and practical or empirical judgments can be clarified by one last glance at the case of the wave poem. Suppose, having seen the second stanza wash up on the beach, you have decided that the "poem" is really an accidental effect of erosion, percolation, and so on and therefore not language at all. What would it now take to change your mind? No theoretical argument will make a difference. But suppose you notice, rising out of the sea some distance from the shore, a small submarine, out of which clamber a half dozen figures in white lab coats. One of them trains his binoculars on the beach and shouts triumphantly, "It worked! It worked! Let's go down and try it again." Presumably, you will now once again change your mind, not because you have a new account of language, meaning, or intention but because you now have new evidence of an author. The question of authorship is and always was an empirical question; it has now received a new empirical answer. The theoretical temptation is to imagine that such empirical questions must, or should, have theoretical answers.

Even a philosopher as committed to the intentional status of language as Searle succumbs to this temptation to think that intention is a theoretical issue. After insisting, in the passage cited earlier, on the inescapability of intention, he goes on to say that "in serious literal speech the sentences are precisely the realizations of the intentions" and that "there need be no *gulf* at all between the illocutionary intention and its expression."[6] The point, however, is not that there *need* be no gulf between intention and the meaning of its expression but that there *can* be no gulf. Not only in serious literal speech but in *all* speech what is intended and what is meant are identical. In separating the two Searle imagines the possibility of expression without intention and so, like Hirsch, misses the point of his own claim that when it comes to language

6. Searle, "Reiterating," p. 202.

"there is no getting away from intentionality." Missing this point, and hence imagining the possibility of two different *kinds* of meaning, is more than a theoretical mistake; it is the sort of mistake that makes theory possible. It makes theory possible because it creates the illusion of a choice between alternative methods of interpreting.[7]

To be a theorist is only to think that there is such a choice. In this respect intentionalists and anti-intentionalists are the same. They are also the same in another respect: neither can really escape intention. But this doesn't mean the intentionalists win, since what intentionalists want is a guide to valid interpretation; what they get, however, is simply a description of what everyone always does. In practical terms, then, the stakes in the battle over intention are extremely low—in fact, they don't exist. Hence it doesn't matter who wins. In theoretical terms, however, the stakes are extremely high, and it still doesn't matter who wins. The stakes are high because they amount to the existence of theory itself; it doesn't matter who wins because as long as one thinks that a position on intention (either for or against) makes a difference in achieving valid interpretations, the ideal of theory itself is saved. Theory wins. But as soon as we recognize that there are no theoretical choices to be made, then the point of theory vanishes. Theory loses.[8]

---

7. In conversation with the authors, Hirsch mentioned the case of a well-known critic and theorist who was persuaded by new evidence that his former reading of a poem was mistaken but who, nevertheless, professed to like his original reading better than what he now admitted was the author's intention. Hirsch meant this example to show the importance of choosing intention over some other interpretive criterion. But the critic in Hirsch's anecdote was not choosing among separate methods of interpretation; he was simply preferring his mistake. Such a preference is surely irrelevant to the theory of interpretation; it might affect what one does *with* an interpretation, but it has no effect on how one *gets* an interpretation.

8. The arguments presented here against theoretical treatments of intention at the local utterance level would apply, virtually unaltered, to accounts of larger-scale intentions elsewhere in Hirsch; they would apply as well to the theoretical proposals of such writers as M. H. Abrams, Wayne C. Booth, R. S. Crane, and Ralph W. Rader—all associated, directly or indirectly, with the Chicago School. Despite variations of approach and emphasis, these writers tend to agree that critical debates about the meaning of a particular passage ought to be resolved through reference to the broader structural intentions informing the work in which the passage appears. Local meanings, in this view, should be deduced from hypothetical constructions of intentions implicit, for example, in an author's choice of genre; these interpretive hypotheses should in turn be confirmed or falsified by their success or failure in explaining the work's details. But this procedure would have methodological force only if the large-scale intentions were different in theoretical status from the local meanings they are supposed to constrain. We would argue, however, that all local meanings are always intentional and that structural choices and local utterances are therefore related to intention in exactly the same fashion. While an interpreter's sense of one might determine his sense of the other, neither is available to interpretation—or amenable to interpretive agreement—in a specially objective way. (Whether interpretations of intention at any level are best conceived as hypotheses is another, though a related, question.)

3. Language and Speech Acts

We have argued that what a text means and what its author intends it to mean are identical and that their identity robs intention of any theoretical interest. A similar account of the relation between meaning and intention has recently been advanced by P. D. Juhl. According to Juhl, "there is a logical connection between statements about the meaning of a literary work and statements about the author's intention such that a statement about the meaning of a work *is* a statement about the author's intention." Juhl criticizes Hirsch, as we do, for believing that critics "*ought* to . . . try to ascertain the author's intention," when in fact, Juhl argues, "they are necessarily doing so already" (*Interpretation*, p. 12). But for Juhl, these claims serve in no way to discredit theory; rather, they themselves constitute a theory that "makes us aware of what we as critics or readers are doing in interpreting literature" and, more crucially, "provides the basis for a principled acceptance or rejection of an interpretation of a literary work" (p. 10). How is it that Juhl derives a theory from arguments which seem to us to make theory impossible?

What makes this question particularly intriguing is the fact that Juhl's strategy for demonstrating the centrality of intention is apparently identical to ours; it consists "in contrasting statements about the meaning of a literary work created by a person with statements about the meaning of a text produced by chance, such as a computer poem" (p. 13).[9] But Juhl's treatment of examples like our wave poem reveals that his sense of the relation between language and intention is after all radically different from ours. Like Hirsch, but at a further level of abstraction, Juhl ends up imagining the possibility of language prior to and independent of intention and thus conceiving intention as something that must be added to language to make it work. Like Hirsch, and like theorists in general, Juhl thinks that intention is a matter of choice. But where Hirsch recommends that we choose intention to adjudicate among interpretations, Juhl thinks no recommendation is necessary—not because we need never choose intention but only because our concept of a literary work is such that to read literature is already to have chosen intention.

Discussing the case of a "poem" produced by chance ("marks on [a] rock" or "a computer poem"), Juhl points out that there is "something odd about *interpreting* [such a] 'text.' " However one might understand this text, one could not understand it as a representation of "the meaning of a particular utterance." We agree with this—if it implies that the

9. In fact, Juhl employs the same poem we do—Wordsworth's "A Slumber Did My Spirit Seal"—in his own treatment of accidental "language" (*Interpretation*, pp. 70–82). The device of contrasting intentional speech acts with marks produced by chance is a familiar one in speech-act theory.

random marks mean nothing, are not language, and therefore cannot be interpreted at all. But for Juhl the implications are different. He thinks that one *can* interpret the random marks, though only in the somewhat specialized sense "in which we might be said to 'interpret' a sentence when we explain its meaning to a foreigner, by explaining to him what the individual words mean, how they function in the sentence, and thus how the sentence *could* be used or what it *could* be used to express or convey" (pp. 84–86).

Our point is that marks produced by chance are not words at all but only resemble them. For Juhl, the marks remain words, but words detached from the intentions that would make them utterances. Thus he can argue that when a "parrot utters the words 'Water is pouring down from the sky,' " one can understand that "the words mean 'It is raining' " but deny that the " 'parrot *said* that it is raining' " (p. 109).[10] It is clear that, for Juhl, the words continue to mean even when devoid of intention. They mean "*in abstracto*" and thus constitute the condition of language prior to the addition of intention, that is, prior to "a speaker's utterance or speech act." In literary interpretation, this condition of language is never operative because, Juhl claims, "our notion of the meaning of a literary work" is "like our notion of the meaning of a person's speech act," not "like our notion of the meaning of a word in a language" (p. 41).[11]

Implicit in Juhl's whole treatment of meaning and intention is the distinction made here between language and speech acts. This distinction makes possible a methodological prescription as strong as Hirsch's, if more general: when confronted with a piece of language, read it as a speech act. The prescriptive force of Juhl's argument is obscured by the fact that he has pushed the moment of decision one step back. Whereas Hirsch thinks we have to add intention to *literature* in order to determine what a text means, Juhl thinks that adding intentions to *language* gives us speech acts (such as literary works) whose meaning is already determinate. Juhl recognizes that as soon as we think of a piece of language as literature, we already regard it as a speech act and hence the product of intention; his prescription tells us how to get from language in general to a specific utterance, such as a literary work.[12]

10. Juhl briefly acknowledges the strangeness of the sort of distinction he makes here when he asks whether words produced by chance could even be called "words" (*Interpretation*, p. 84). But he drops the question as abruptly as he raises it.

11. For additional remarks on meaning "*in abstracto*," see Juhl, *Interpretation*, pp. 25 n, 55–57, 203, 223, 238, 288–89.

12. Juhl's motives are, in fact, not far from Hirsch's. For both theorists, meaning *in abstracto* is indeterminate or ambiguous ("indeterminate" for Hirsch, "ambiguous" for Juhl); both appeal to intention in order to achieve determinate or particular meanings or, as Juhl says, to "disambiguate" the text (*Interpretation*, p. 97). This theoretical interest in the problem of indeterminacy derives in part from the widespread notion that words and sentences have a range of "linguistically possible" meanings, the ones recorded in dic-

But this prescription only makes sense if its two terms (language and speech acts) are not already inseparable in the same way that meaning and intention are. Juhl is right of course to claim that marks without intention are not speech acts, since the essence of a speech act is its intentional character. But we have demonstrated that marks without intention are not language either. Only by failing to see that linguistic meaning is always identical to expressed intention can Juhl imagine language without speech acts. To recognize the identity of language and speech acts is to realize that Juhl's prescription—when confronted with language, read it as a speech act—can mean nothing more than: when confronted with language, read it as language.

For Hirsch and Juhl, the goal of theory is to provide an objectively valid method of literary interpretation. To make method possible, both are forced to imagine intentionless meanings or, in more general terms, to imagine a separation between language and speech acts.[13] The method then consists in adding speech acts to language; speech acts bring with them the particular intentions that allow interpreters to clear up the ambiguities intrinsic to language as such. But this separation of language and speech acts need not be used to establish an interpretive method; it can in fact be used to do just the opposite. For a theorist like Paul de Man, the priority of language to speech acts suggests that all attempts to arrive at determinate meanings by adding intentions amount to a violation of the genuine condition of language. If theory in its positive or methodological mode rests on the choice of speech acts over language, theory in its negative or antimethodological mode tries to preserve what it takes to be the purity of language from the distortion of speech acts.

The negative theorist's hostility to method depends on a particular account of language, most powerfully articulated in de Man's "The Purloined Ribbon." The essay concerns what de Man sees as a crucial episode in Rousseau's *Confessions*, in which Rousseau attempts to interpret, and thereby to justify, a particularly incriminating speech act. While working as a servant, he had stolen a ribbon from his employers.

---

tionaries and grammar books. But a dictionary is an index of frequent usages in particular speech acts—not a matrix of abstract, pre-intentional possibilities. (For Hirsch's terminological distinction between ambiguity and indeterminacy, see *Validity in Interpretation*, p. 230.)

13. This distinction, in one form or another, is common among speech-act theorists. H. P. Grice, for example, distinguishes between "locutions of the form 'U (utterer) meant that . . .'" and "locutions of the form 'X (utterance-type) means . . . ,'" characterizing the first as "occasion-meaning" and the second as "applied timeless meaning" (H. P. Grice, "Utterer's Meaning, Sentence-Meaning, and Word-Meaning," in *The Philosophy of Language*, ed. Searle [London, 1971], pp. 54–56). And Searle, citing Wittgenstein ("*Say* 'it's cold here' and *mean* 'it's warm here' "), distinguishes between meaning as a "matter of intention" and meaning as a "matter of convention" (*Speech Acts* [Cambridge, 1969], p. 45).

When accused of the theft, he blamed it on a fellow servant, Marion. In the passage that interests de Man, Rousseau is thus concerned with two crimes, the theft itself and the far more heinous act of excusing himself by accusing an innocent girl. This second act, the naming of Marion, is the one that especially needs justifying.

Rousseau offers several excuses, each an explanation of what he meant by naming Marion. But the explanation that intrigues de Man is the surprising one that Rousseau perhaps meant nothing at all when he said "Marion." He was merely uttering the first sound that occurred to him: "Rousseau was making whatever noise happened to come into his head; he was saying nothing at all."[14] Hence, de Man argues, "In the spirit of the text, one should resist all temptation to give any significance whatever to the sound 'Marion.' " The claim that "Marion" was meaningless gives Rousseau his best defense: "For it is only if . . . the utterance of the sound 'Marion' is truly without any conceivable motive that the total arbitrariness of the action becomes the most effective, the most efficaciously performative excuse of all" (p. 37). Why? Because, "if the essential non-signification of the statement had been properly interpreted, if Rousseau's accusers had realized that Marion's name was 'le premier objet qui s'offrit,' they would have understood his lack of guilt as well as Marion's innocence" (p. 40).

But de Man is less interested in the efficacy of the "excuse" than he is in what it reveals about the fundamental nature of language. The fact that the sound "Marion" can mean nothing reminds us that language consists of inherently meaningless sounds to which one adds meanings—in other words, that the relation between signifier and signified is arbitrary. Why does de Man think this apparently uncontroversial description of language has any theoretical interest? The recognition that the material condition of language is inherently meaningless has no theoretical force in itself. But de Man thinks that the material condition of language is not simply meaningless but is also already "linguistic," that is, sounds are signifiers even before meanings (signifieds) are added to them. As a collection of "pure signifier[s]," in themselves "devoid of meaning and function," language is primarily a meaningless structure to which meanings are secondarily (and in de Man's view illegitimately) added (p. 32). Thus, according to de Man, Rousseau's accusers mistakenly added a meaning to the signifier "Marion"—hearing a speech act where they should have heard only language. This separation of language and speech act is the precondition for de Man's version of the theoretical choice.

De Man's separation of language and speech acts rests on a mistake. It is of course true that sounds in themselves are meaningless. It is also

14. Paul de Man, "The Purloined Ribbon," *Glyph* 1 (1977): 39; all further citations to this work will be included in the text.

true that sounds become signifiers when they function in language. But it is not true that sounds in themselves are signifiers; they become signifiers only when they acquire meanings, and when they lose their meanings they stop being signifiers. De Man's mistake is to think that the sound "Marion" remains a signifier even when emptied of all meaning.[15] The fact is that the meaningless noise "Marion" only *resembles* the signifier "Marion," just as accidentally uttering the sound "Marion" only *resembles* the speech act of naming Marion. De Man recognizes that the accidental emission of the sound "Marion" is not a speech act (indeed, that's the point of the example), but he fails to recognize that it's not language either. What reduces the signifier to noise and the speech act to an accident is the absence of intention. Conceiving linguistic activity as the accidental emission of phonemes, de Man arrives at a vision of "the absolute randomness of language, prior to any figuration or meaning": "There can be no use of language which is not, within a certain perspective thus radically formal, i.e. mechanical, no matter how deeply this aspect may be concealed by aesthetic, formalistic delusions" (pp. 44, 41).

By conceiving language as essentially random and mechanical, de Man gives a new response to the dilemma of the wave poem and suggests a fuller account of why that dilemma is central to theory in general. Our earlier discussion of the wave poem was intended to show how counterintuitive it is to separate language and intention. When the second stanza washed up on the beach, even the theorist should have been ready to admit that the poem was not a poem because the marks were not language. But our subsequent discussions of Juhl and de Man have revealed that theory precisely depends on not making this admission. For Juhl, the accidental marks remain language, but language *in abstracto* and hence inherently ambiguous. The wave poem thus presents a positive theorist like Juhl with a choice between the multiple meanings of intentionless marks and the determinate meaning of an intentional speech act. Since the point of positive theory is to ground the practice of determining particular meanings, the positive theorist chooses to read the marks as an intentional act. But when a negative theorist like de Man encounters the second (accidental) stanza, it presents him with a slightly different version of the same choice. For de Man the marks are not multiply meaningful but essentially meaningless, and the choice is not between one intentional meaning and many intentionless meanings but between intentional meaning and no meaning at all. Since, in de Man's view, all imputations of meaning are equally groundless, the positive theorist's choice of intention seems to him pointless. In apparent hostility

15. Another, perhaps more usual, way of reaching this notion of the pure signifier is by observing that one signifier can be attached to many different meanings and concluding from this that the signifier has an identity of its own, independent of meaning in general. But the conclusion doesn't follow. Far from attaining its true identity when unrelated to any meaning, a signifier in this condition merely ceases to be a signifier.

to interpretive method, the negative theorist chooses the meaningless marks. But the negative theorist's choice in fact provides him with a positive methodology, a methodology that grounds the practice of interpretation in the single decisive truth about language. The truth about language is its accidental and mechanical nature: any text, "properly interpreted," will reveal its "essential nonsignification" (p. 40). For both Juhl and de Man, proper interpretation depends upon following a methodological prescription. Juhl's prescription is: when confronted with language, read it as a speech act. De Man's prescription is: when confronted with what seems to be a speech act, read it as language.

The wave poem, as encountered by a theorist, presents a choice between two kinds of meaning or, what comes to the same thing, two kinds of language. The issue in both cases is the presence or absence of intention; the positive theorist adds intention, the negative theorist subtracts it.[16] In our view, however, the relation between meaning and intention or, in slightly different terms, between language and speech acts is such that intention can neither be added nor subtracted. Intention cannot be added to or subtracted from meaning because meanings are always intentional; intention cannot be added to or subtracted from language because language consists of speech acts, which are also always intentional. Since language has intention already built into it, no recommendation about what to do with intention has any bearing on the question of how to interpret any utterance or text. For the nontheorist, the only question raised by the wave poem is not *how* to interpret but *whether* to interpret. Either the marks are a poem and hence a speech act, or they are not a poem and just happen to resemble a speech act. But once this empirical question is decided, no further judgments—and therefore no theoretical judgments—about the status of intention can be made.

4. Theory and Practice

Our argument so far has concerned what might be called the ontological side of theory—its peculiar claims about the nature of its object. We have suggested that those claims always take the form of generating a difference where none in fact exists, by imagining a mode of language devoid of intention—devoid, that is, of what makes it language and distinguishes it from accidental or mechanical noises and marks. But we have also tried to show that this strange ontological project is more than a spontaneous anomaly; it is always in the service of an epistemological

16. At least this is true of the present generation of theorists. For earlier theorists such as W. K. Wimsatt and Monroe C. Beardsley, the objective meanings sought by positive theory were to be acquired precisely by *subtracting* intention and relying on the formal rules and public norms of language. This, of course, is the view they urge in "The Intentional Fallacy" (*The Verbal Icon: Studies in the Meaning of Poetry* [Lexington, Ky., 1954], pp. 3–18).

goal. That goal is the goal of method, the governance of interpretive practice by some larger and more principled account. Indeed, theoretical controversy in the Anglo-American tradition has more often taken the form of arguments about the epistemological situation of the interpreter than about the ontological status of the text. If the ontological project of theory has been to imagine a condition of language before intention, its epistemological project has been to imagine a condition of knowledge before interpretation.

The aim of theory's epistemological project is to base interpretation on a direct encounter with its object, an encounter undistorted by the influence of the interpreter's particular beliefs. Several writers have demonstrated the impossibility of escaping beliefs at any stage of interpretation and have concluded that theory's epistemological goal is therefore unattainable. Some have gone on to argue that the unattainability of an epistemologically neutral stance not only undermines the claims of method but prevents us from ever getting any correct interpretations. For these writers the attack on method thus has important practical consequences for literary criticism, albeit negative ones.[17]

But in discussing theory from the ontological side, we have tried to suggest that the impossibility of method has no practical consequences, positive or negative. And the same conclusion has been reached from the epistemological side by the strongest critic of theoretical attempts to escape belief, Stanley Fish. In his last essay in *Is There a Text in This Class?*, Fish confronts the "final question" raised by his critique of method, namely, "what implications it has for the practice of literary criticism." His answer is, "none whatsoever":

> That is, it does not follow from what I have been saying that you should go out and do literary criticism in a certain way or refrain from doing it in other ways. The reason for this is that the position I have been presenting is not one that you (or anyone else) could live by. Its thesis is that whatever seems to you to be obvious and inescapable is only so within some institutional or conventional structure, and that means that you can never operate outside some such structure, even if you are persuaded by the thesis. As soon as you descend from theoretical reasoning about your assumptions, you will once again inhabit them and you will inhabit them without any reservations whatsoever; so that when you are called on to talk

17. Negative theory rests on the perception of what de Man calls "an insurmountable obstacle in the way of any reading or understanding" (*Allegories of Reading* [New Haven, Conn., 1979], p. 131). Some theorists (e.g., David Bleich and Norman Holland) understand this obstacle as the reader's subjectivity. Others (like de Man himself and J. Hillis Miller) understand it as the aporia between constative and performative language, between demonstration and persuasion. In all cases, however, the negative theorist is committed to the view that interpretation is, as Jonathan Culler says, "necessary error" (*The Pursuit of Signs* [Ithaca, N.Y., 1981], p. 14).

about Milton or Wordsworth or Yeats, you will do so from within whatever beliefs you hold about these authors.[18]

At the heart of this passage is the familiar distinction between "theoretical reasoning" and the "assumptions" or "beliefs" that inform the concrete "practice of literary criticism." Where most theorists affirm the practical importance of their theories, Fish's originality lies in his denial that his theory has any practical consequences whatsoever. But once theory gives up all claims to affect practice, what is there left for theory to do? Or, since Fish's point is that there is nothing left for theory to *do,* what is there left for theory to *be?* Understood in these terms, Fish's work displays the theoretical impulse in its purest form. Stripped of the methodological project either to ground or to undermine practice, theory continues to imagine a position outside it. While this retreat to a position outside practice looks like theory's last desperate attempt to save itself, it is really, as we hope to show, the founding gesture of all theoretical argument.

Fish's attack on method begins with an account of belief that is in our view correct. The account's two central features are, first, the recognition that beliefs cannot be grounded in some deeper condition of knowledge and, second, the further recognition that this impossibility does not in any way weaken their claims to be true. "If one believes what one believes," Fish writes, "then one believes that what one believes is *true,* and conversely, one believes that what one doesn't believe is not true" (p. 361). Since one can neither escape one's beliefs nor escape the sense that they are true, Fish rejects both the claims of method and the claims of skepticism. Methodologists and skeptics maintain that the validity of beliefs depends on their being grounded in a condition of knowledge prior to and independent of belief; they differ only about whether this is possible. The virtue of Fish's account is that it shows why an insistence on the inescapability of belief is in no way inimical to the ordinary notions of truth and falsehood implicit in our sense of what knowledge is. The character of belief is precisely what gives us those notions in the first place; having beliefs just *is* being committed to the truth of what one believes and the falsehood of what one doesn't believe. But to say all this is, as Fish asserts, to offer no practical help or hindrance to the task of acquiring true beliefs. We can no more get true beliefs by looking for knowledge than we can get an author's meaning by looking for his or her intention, and for the same reason: knowledge and true belief are the same.

So far, this argument seems to us flawless. But Fish, as it turns out,

18. Stanley Fish, *Is There a Text in This Class?: The Authority of Interpretive Communities* (Cambridge, Mass., 1980), p. 370; all further citations to this work will be included in the text.

fails to recognize the force of his own discussion of belief, and this failure is what makes him a theorist. It commits him, ultimately, to the ideal of knowledge implicit in all epistemological versions of theory, and it leads him to affirm, after all, the methodological value of his theoretical stance. Fish's departure from his account of belief shows up most vividly in his response to charges that his arguments lead to historical relativism. The fear of relativism is a fear that the abandonment of method must make all inquiry pointless. But, Fish rightly says, inquiry never seems pointless; our present beliefs about an object always seem better than any previous beliefs about the same object: "In other words, the idea of progress is inevitable, not, however, because there *is* a progress in the sense of a clearer and clearer sight of an independent object but because the *feeling* of having progressed is an inevitable consequence of the firmness with which we hold our beliefs" (pp. 361–62).

As an account of the inevitable psychology of belief, this is irreproachable. But when he later turns from the general issue of intellectual progress to the particular case of progress in literary criticism, Fish makes clear that he thinks our psychological assurance is unfounded. Our present beliefs only *seem* better than earlier ones; they never really *are*. And, indeed, the discovery of this truth about our beliefs gives us, Fish thinks, a new understanding of the history of literary criticism and a new sense of how to go about studying it. According to what Fish calls the "old model" for making sense of the history of criticism, the work of critics "like Sidney, Dryden, Pope, Coleridge, Arnold" could only be seen as "the record of the rather dismal performances of men . . . who simply did not understand literature and literary values as well as we do." But Fish's new model enables us to "regard those performances not as unsuccessful attempts to approximate our own but as extensions of a literary culture whose assumptions were *not inferior but merely different*" (pp. 367–68; our emphasis).

To imagine that we can see the beliefs we hold as no better than but "merely different" from opposing beliefs held by others is to imagine a position from which we can see our beliefs without really believing them. To be in this position would be to see the truth about beliefs without actually having any—to know without believing. In the moment in which he imagines this condition of knowledge outside belief, Fish has forgotten the point of his own earlier identification of knowledge and true belief.

Once a theorist has reached this vision of knowledge, there are two epistemological ways to go: realism and idealism. A realist thinks that theory allows us to stand outside our beliefs in a neutral encounter with the objects of interpretation; an idealist thinks that theory allows us to stand outside our beliefs in a neutral encounter with our beliefs themselves. The issue in both cases is the relation between objects and beliefs.

For the realist, the object exists independent of beliefs, and knowledge requires that we shed our beliefs in a disinterested quest for the object. For the idealist, who insists that we can never shed our beliefs, knowledge means recognizing the role beliefs play in *constituting* their objects. Fish, with his commitment to the primacy of beliefs, chooses idealism: "objects," he thinks, "are made and not found"; interpretation "is not the art of construing but the art of constructing" (pp. 331, 327). Once he arrives at epistemological idealism, Fish's methodological payoff immediately follows. Knowing that "interpreters do not decode poems" but "make them," "we are free to consider the various forms the literary institution has taken and to uncover the interpretative strategies by which its canons have been produced and understood" (pp. 327, 368). By thinking of the critic as an idealist instead of a realist, Fish is able to place literary criticism at the very center of all literary practice:

> No longer is the critic the humble servant of texts whose glories exist independently of anything he might do; it is what he does, within the constraints embedded in the literary institution, that brings texts into being and makes them available for analysis and appreciation. The practice of literary criticism is not something one must apologize for; it is absolutely essential not only to the maintenance of, but to the very production of, the objects of its attention. [P. 368]

We began this section by noting that Fish, like us, thinks that no general account of belief can have practical consequences. But, as we have just seen, *his* account turns out to have consequences after all. Why, then, is Fish led both to assert that his argument has no practical consequences and to proclaim its importance in providing a new model for critical practice? The answer is that, despite his explicit disclaimers, he thinks a true account of belief must be a *theory* about belief, whereas we think a true account of belief can only be a *belief* about belief.[19] The difference between these two senses of what it means to have a true account of something is the difference between theory and the kind of pragmatist argument we are presenting here. These two kinds of positions conceive their inconsequentiality in two utterly different ways. A belief about the nature of beliefs is inconsequential because it merely tells you what beliefs are, not whether they are true or false in particular or in general. From this point of view, knowing the truth about belief will no more help you in acquiring true beliefs than knowing that meaning is intentional will help you find correct meanings. This is not in the least to

19. Fish calls his account a "general or metacritical belief " (*Is There a Text in This Class?*, p. 359; cf. pp. 368–70).

say that you can't have true beliefs, only that you can't get them by having a good account of what beliefs are.

Fish's *theory* about beliefs, on the other hand, strives to achieve inconsequentiality by standing outside all the practical commitments that belief entails. It is perfectly true that one can achieve inconsequentiality by going outside beliefs but only because, as Fish himself insists, to be outside beliefs is to be nowhere at all. But of course Fish doesn't think that his theory about beliefs leaves him nowhere at all; he thinks instead that it gives him a way of arriving at truth, not by choosing some beliefs over others but by choosing beliefless knowledge over all beliefs. The truth of knowledge, according to Fish, is that no beliefs are, in the long run, truer than others; all beliefs, in the long run, are equal. But, as we have noted, it is only from the standpoint of a theory about belief which is not itself a belief that this truth can be seen. Hence the descent from "theoretical reasoning" about our beliefs to the actual practice of believing—from neutrality to commitment—demands that we forget the truth theory has told us. Unlike the ordinary methodologist, Fish wants to repudiate the attempt to derive practice from theory, insisting that the world of practice must be founded not on theoretical truth but on the repression of theoretical truth. But the sense that practice can only begin with the repression of theory already amounts to a methodological prescription: when confronted with beliefs, forget that they are not really true. This prescription gives Fish everything theory always wants: knowledge of the truth-value of beliefs and instructions on what to do with them.[20]

We can now see why Fish, in the first passage quoted, says that his position is "not one that you (or anyone else) could live by . . . even if you [were] persuaded" by it. Theory, he thinks, can have no practical consequences; it cannot be lived because theory and practice—the truth about belief and belief itself—can never in principle be united. In our view, however, the only relevant truth about belief is that you can't go outside it, and, far from being unlivable, this is a truth you can't help but live. It has no practical consequences not because it can never be *united* with practice but because it can never be *separated* from practice.

The theoretical impulse, as we have described it, always involves the attempt to separate things that should not be separated: on the ontological side, meaning from intention, language from speech acts; on the epistemological side, knowledge from true belief. Our point has been that the separated terms are in fact inseparable. It is tempting to end by saying that theory and practice too are inseparable. But this would be a mistake. Not because theory and practice (unlike the other terms) really

20. In one respect Fish's prescription is unusual: it separates the two theoretical goals of grounding practice and reaching objective truth. It tells us what is true and how to behave—but not how to behave in order to find out what is true.

are separate but because theory is nothing else but the attempt to escape practice. Meaning is just another name for expressed intention, knowledge just another name for true belief, but theory is not just another name for practice. It is the name for all the ways people have tried to stand outside practice in order to govern practice from without. Our thesis has been that no one can reach a position outside practice, that theorists should stop trying, and that the theoretical enterprise should therefore come to an end.

Revisionary Madness: The Prospects of American Literary Theory at the Present Time

Daniel T. O'Hara

> For if I triumph I must make men mad.
> —W. B. YEATS, "The Tower"

1

Now must be the time to turn our backs on literary theory. Signs are everywhere that such a move would be advisable. Such distinctive American theorists as Harold Bloom, Stanley Fish, and Edward Said, each for his own reasons, have recently warned the critical community about the dangers of doing theory in a post-structuralist mode. Everyone now knows or should know what M. H. Abrams and Gerald Graff—to identify just two of the more prominent and persistent opponents of theory—have been saying for years. The elusive, purely theoretical quest for the hidden rules governing *the system* of production, dissemination, and interpretation of texts, a quest generally informed by an essential concern to revise the academic study of literature, can lead only to the foolish positing of some single, all-determining principle of critical practice (Language, Power, Influence, etc.)—that is, to a speculative trap of self-indulgent rarefaction, in short, to an intellectual dead end. For the notion of there being a "system" reducible to a single magical formula is

I wish to thank the Mellon Foundation of the University of Pittsburgh and the department of English for their generous support in order to write this essay. In addition, I must acknowledge my great debt to a colleague of mine at Temple University, Linda Rubin, with whom I have discussed the general issues involved in living in an era of "revisionary madness." Such discussions were enormously helpful to me.

Reprinted from the June 1983 issue of *Critical Inquiry*.

at best a hypothetical construct and at worst each theorist's fetching chimera, the fantastic image of his possible sublimity, his will to power over other theorists writ large and alone in the intense inane. In this light, doing theory now, in however self-conscious and ironic a fashion, would represent a radical and wasteful break with the American tradition of pragmatically oriented, intellectually skeptical, and socially aware (if politically uncommitted) scholar-critics.[1]

This strange turnabout, in which the leading literary theorists and their disciples join hands with representatives of the loyal, neo-humanist opposition, is a paradox. It even smacks of the willfully perverse.[2] As I observe this spectacle of a new antitheoretical consensus forming right before my eyes, the question that strikes me is this: Why should American literary theorists—marginal figures with respect to the larger culture—appear to be so determined to wipe themselves out of the picture entirely, so to speak, just as they are witnessing the first fruits of their labors to institutionalize theory as a subdiscipline within the critical profession?

For one of the most immediately accessible examples of this revisionary exercise of turning against theory—one that, for me, suggests a plausible answer to my question—consider the following conclusion on the dangerous delusions of theory made recently in "Against Theory" by Steven Knapp and Walter Benn Michaels, two of theory's most perceptive students: Theory "is the name for all the ways people have tried to stand outside practice in order to govern practice from without. Our thesis has been that no one can reach a position outside practice, that theorists should stop trying, and that the theoretical enterprise should therefore come to an end" (p. 30).[3] What is one to make of this provocative and deeply problematic conclusion?

1. See, e.g., Harold Bloom, *Agon: Towards a Theory of Revisionism* (New York, 1982), pp. 16–51; Stanley Fish, *Is There a Text in This Class?: The Authority of Interpretive Communities* (Cambridge, Mass., 1980); Edward W. Said, "Travelling Theory," *Raritan* 1 (Winter 1982): 41–67; M. H. Abrams, "The Deconstructive Angel," *Critical Inquiry* 3 (Spring 1977): esp. 426–29; and Gerald Graff, *Literature against Itself* (Chicago, 1979).

2. The situation is so bad as to provoke Paul de Man to write a book on the topic, *The Resistance to Theory;* an important piece from it has recently been published in *The Pedagogical Imperative: Teaching as a Literary Genre, Yale French Studies* 63 (1982): 3–20.

3. I am not concerned with all the particulars of their argument; rather it is the overall rhetorical strategy and effect that concern me. To borrow Bloom's notion, their essay in its entirely negative stance embodies the latecomer's resentful psychology rather too clearly.

Daniel T. O'Hara, associate professor of English at Temple University and an assistant editor of *Boundary 2,* is the author of *Tragic Knowledge: Yeats's Autobiography and Hermeneutics,* coeditor of *The Question of Textuality: Strategies of Reading in Contemporary American Criticism,* and editor of a special issue of *Boundary 2, Why Nietzsche Now?*

The point that Knapp and Michaels make is an important one, especially in these revisionary days of Reaganomics and other such ills. They reach their conclusion after arguing that in order to get the theoretical project off the ground and then keep it aloft, the theorist, no matter what his stripe, whether he is an intentionalist like E. D. Hirsch and P. D. Juhl or a deconstructive ironist like Paul de Man and Fish, must assume that some "ultimate" vantage point beyond the discursive field under scrutiny can in principle be envisioned and separated out from the realm of practice and what they call "true belief."[4] Only if the theorist assumes that such a synoptic view and such an apocalyptic separation are possible (even if that view is of the abyss and that separation is really a self-incarceration) can the theorist pretend to knowledge and so to a command of the underlying rules governing the field. Whatever such "knowledge" may portend—man's freedom or some depersonalizing fate at the hands of Power, Language, or Precursor—makes little practical difference to the success of the theoretical project. The only thing that matters is the theorist's belief in his prospects of attaining that all-determining higher ground, however "fictional" that position is programmatically said to be by any particular theorist.

Clearly, Knapp and Michaels do not believe that such a vantage point is possible and, furthermore, that belief in such a possibility is anything more than an act of bad faith, whether made in the good taste of ironic self-consciousness or not. Consequently, for them, questions like whether man masters language or language masters man are meaningless, akin to the theosophists' disputes about the possibility of the dead experiencing sensual pleasure in the afterlife. In this respect, Knapp and Michaels follow Fish. For their master Fish, all objectivist, idealist, or transcendental tendencies to posit a position beyond the strident intricacies of critical practice and its wars of true belief are merely projections of the theorist's desire for such an ideal vantage point. This is the case, for Fish, no matter how hedged about such tendencies may be by ironic qualifications, opaque terminologies, and deconstructive posturings. Such tendencies, then, produce a wish-fulfilling bit of phantasmagoria, a dream of escape from the arid conflicts involved in the actual world of strenuous critical argument. One needs relief, so one simply spells it "o-a-s-i-s," or "i-s-l-a-n-d," or "t-o-w-e-r."[5]

But Knapp and Michaels do not stop with their repetition of Fish. They go on to claim that he who originally made possible their critical insight into the mechanisms of theory-production has recently suffered

4. The sources for their notion of "true belief" are various. Hans Gadamer's idea of "prejudice," for example, comes to mind. The point is that if one did a genealogy of their ideas one would discover that their position against theory depends entirely on assumptions that are theoretical.

5. Or "t-h-e-o-r-y."

an acute lapse from his formerly rigorous position.[6] By trying to
establish his view of the reader's share in the constitution of the text as
the best theory of interpretation, Fish has attempted to set up his hermeneutics (and so himself as well) as the governing principle of media-
tion operating among the different conflicting interpretive communities.
Knapp and Michaels contend, therefore, that Fish, who had once assumed he could eradicate the crime of critical theory—with the help of
his ironic theory of the reader's imaginative response to the self-
consuming text—has instead perpetuated that crime. After using Fish to
deconstruct Juhl and de Man and, in turn, using Fish's own arguments
to deconstruct Fish himself, Knapp and Michaels, true to their principle
of repressing "the theoretical impulse," refuse to offer a theory—or
even an antitheory—of their own to account adequately for either the
interpretive practices they have partially discussed or those they have
implicitly employed. Instead, as seen by their conclusion, they end up
calling for the death of theory. Or it might be more appropriate to say
that they retreat from the sublime abyss (or is it the revisionary void?)
and offer to the poor pathetic figure of the literary theorist a good old
hefty, Anglo-Saxon broad sword upon which to fall: "Despite his explicit
disclaimers, [Fish] thinks a true account of belief must be a *theory* about
belief, whereas we think a true account of belief can only be a *belief* about
belief" (p. 28).

This ironic spectacle of "the self-dispatching genius," quite explicit
here, is now being staged repeatedly throughout the profession, with
more or less subtlety, for other theorists by their former students and
allies.[7] I point to this development not to blame or to praise anyone. Nor
am I interested in the phenomenon as a clue to new trends in intellectual
fashions. Rather, I find this recent oppositon to theory representative of
the manner in which the revisionary imagination operates generally in
our "post-modern" culture. That is, it exhausts, virtually as it opens up,
those all-too-briefly viable alternatives of intellectual production outside
the normal range of conventional procedures. In light of this ironic style
of the revisionary imagination, I want to propose a deliberately dramatic
analogy between revisionism and madness, a self-mocking "theory" of
their mutually penetrating interplay. I do so not so much to explain
Knapp and Michaels or others away as to offer provocation in return.
What follows, then, is meant to be taken as a caricature of the revisionary
imagination of American literary theorists.

6. Whether or not Knapp and Michaels' argument against Fish is at all plausible is not
my concern. I suspect that he will take care of his own defense.
7. For one of the best discussions of this recent development, see Paul A. Bové,
"Intellectuals at War: Michel Foucault and the Analytics of Power," in a forthcoming issue
of *Sub-stance*. Bové analyzes Said's recent criticism of Michel Foucault (see n. 1) as a representative case.

2

Schopenhauer in *The World as Will and Representation* characterizes madness as a traumatic derangement of the memory. In so doing, he provides us with a useful analogy for the more extreme forms of the revisionary imagination as they appear throughout modern culture. The madman, according to the great pessimist, remembers the past only in a highly selective, discontinuous manner, while the future appears to him as a looming blank. Ironically enough, the present appears to him more or less exactly as it does to the rest of us. As a result of his memory lapses, the madman must invent an illusory continuity for himself and an illusory context for everyone else, a textual identity and a textual world, essentially metaphorical and associative in nature and wholly rhetorical in effect. As he fills up the gaps in his memory with consoling or terrifying fictions and presses them into service, the madman begins to take these unsuccessful transfigurations of certain unbearable aspects of an irrational reality for "truthful" (i.e., "pragmatically" useful) representations of a (to him) ultimately comprehensible world. Such mad inventions quickly fall into one of two basic pathological categories: that of the melancholic's ruling obsession or fixed idea; or that of the maniac's or fool's purely random improvisations. "The madman," Schopenhauer remarks, "always carries about in his faculty of reason a past in the abstract, but it is a false past that exists for him alone, and that either all the time or merely for the moment. The influence of this false past then prevents the use of the correctly known present."[8] Like Freud after him, Schopenhauer traces in psychological terms a mode of interpretive activity that informs the shape and significance of critical practices.

One could argue, then, that each would-be revisionist structures his reading of a particular precursor or of an entire tradition of precursors in such a way as to suggest that at a certain point in the precursor's writing career or in the development of a tradition, he or the tradition went wrong and started to resemble Schopenhauer's madman.[9] That is, the precursor or tradition begins to become, for the revisionist, a dangerously destructive, even self-destructive, influence that either cannot be contained or rehabilitated without resorting to exorbitant, even violent, interpretive measures.

Thus the more systematic and theoretical the revisionist, the more he appears to be like the chronically anxious melancholic trotting out his master obsession at every opportunity so as to provoke and then ward

8. Arthur Schopenhauer, *The World as Will and Representation*, trans. E. F. J. Payne, 2 vols. (New York, 1966), 1:193.

9. Bloom's revisionary theory of the anxiety of influence is the closest contemporary notion, as Bloom himself knows; see esp. his *Poetry and Repression: Revisionism from Blake to Stevens* (New Haven, Conn., 1976).

off another saving attack of his self-defining anxiety. The more practically oriented "pluralistic" interpreter, who makes the most of all critical means, would accordingly become the pure fool or jolly maniac. And, of course, one can imagine some really "disturbed" critic, with little or no identity of his own—a monster of deconstructive irony, moving "playfully" between these dialectical extremes. In any event, no matter how one construes the underlying conditions for this process—whether in figures drawn from individual psychology, communal ideology, economic theory and practice, or the various histories of institutions, disciplines, and cultures—the textual consequences and the rhetorical effects appear to be the same: in case after case, the critical reader witnesses in the revisionist's text the past being condemned in the name of an enlightened ideal of "liberation" or "sanity" that is to be fully realized in some future time; this ideal, humanistic, even utopian in its dimensions, is derived by the revisionist from what are, ironically enough, essentially literary images lifted out of an even earlier fabulous or mythic past.[10] In other, more metaphorical words, the dialectic of modern revisionism runs the gamut from Don Quixote inflation to Sancho Panza reduction and back again, without any apparent end in sight. In Nietzsche's prophetic words from *Zarathustra,* words which as sublime parody illustrate perfectly both the pattern I have described and the appropriate attitude to it, "Not only the reason of millennia, but their madness, too, breaks out in us."[11]

I don't think that the point has to be belabored. In "Against Theory" Knapp and Michaels, no matter what their intentions, act rhetorically like so many others these days, in a manner that suggests Schopenhauer's understanding of madness as a systematic derangement of the memory. Knapp and Michaels selectively recall portions of texts by Juhl, de Man, and Fish and fill in the gaps between them with their own cleverly argued inventions, drawn from various incompatible and generally unnamed sources (Gadamer, Foucault, Bloom, etc.), all so that they can point out exactly where the critical theorist repeatedly goes wrong. In this way they can make a "valid" call for him to close up shop. What they have done, in order to triumph over their tradition, is to revise it into oblivion.[12] But their triumph is a hollow one, since in place of it they offer only the same old spectacle of critical practice we have known for years. It is as if in fulfilling the dialectical pattern of re-

10. For a discussion of this dialectic of revisionism as it works itself out in deconstructive and Marxist critical texts, see my review of *The Political Unconscious* by Fredric Jameson and *Saving the Text* by Geoffrey Hartman, "The Ideology of Romance," *Comparative Literature* 23 (Summer 1982): 381–89.

11. Friedrich Nietzsche, *Thus Spoke Zarathustra, The Portable Nietzsche,* trans. and ed. Walter Kaufmann (New York, 1954), p. 189.

12. For a further analysis of this self-destructive psychology, see my "The Prophet of Our Laughter: Or Nietzsche as—Educator?," *Boundary 2* 9 (Spring-Fall 1981): 1–19.

visionary interpretation, by playing in their essay the Panzaic critics to
the entire tradition of Quixotic theorists, Knapp and Michaels have de-
stroyed the world of their fathers, only to return us to that of our grand-
fathers, the world of the New Critics and the gentleman-scholars of
literary history (that is, the world of true belief par excellence, before the
advent of Northrop Frye). The irony of such a fulfillment is, of course,
Knapp and Michaels would not fit into such a world.[13]

The effect of their polemic is that it leaves the field open to the
long-established and well-heeled, native American, fly-by-the-seat-of-
one's-pants critical pragmatists and know-nothings, who have been
waiting in the wings ever since the late sixties for such boring annoyances
as critical theory, feminism, affirmative action programs, and so forth to
disappear; we then can go back to doing business as usual, waging our
polite and sensible battles over the sources and significances of some line
in Pound's *Pisan Cantos* or Joyce's manuscript drafts of *Finnegans Wake*.[14]
I am not saying that Knapp and Michaels consciously intend, as Richard
Rorty apparently does, to take us back to John Dewey, William James,
and "Ol' Virginie," only that the effect of their argument, especially on
students, is likely to make unavailable, or at least less attractive and ever
so much more difficult, a career option that has only recently been
introduced in the profession and that has been so strenuously fought
for—namely, doing critical theory.[15] It is almost as if the attitude informing their essay were: "Well, we are making places for ourselves, so
the hell with all those coming after us." But perhaps this is too harsh a
characterization, and their attitude would be better characterized as that
of a latter-day Samson in the temple of his enemies, blind, self-
destructively powerful, and full of the Lord's righteous anger at all the
degradation he senses around (and in) him. I suppose, however, that
whether the antitheoretical impulse underlying the essay is cynical or
moral makes little practical difference. For the rhetorical effect is
essentially nihilistic, and so even in the best possible light the essay aids
and comforts the champions of the status quo.

Yet even this conclusion would not be so bad. After all, we have been
living so long with one apocalyptic nihilism after another appearing in
our culture that one more hardly seems to matter. The problem with
Knapp and Michaels' argument lies in its antidemocratic, genius-will-out
assumption that one can just do criticism. What they fail to realize is that
by clearing the air of theory they have also taken away from students the

13. Their continued interest in questions of theoretical implication suggests as much.
This seems especially true of Michaels; see, e.g., his "Is There a Politics of Interpretation?,"
Critical Inquiry 9 (Sept. 1982): 248–58.
14. For the most succinct history of recent criticism, see A. Walton Litz, "Literary
Criticism," in *Harvard Guide to Contemporary American Writing*, ed. Daniel Hoffman (Cambridge, Mass., 1979), pp. 51–83.
15. For the most virulent form of this return to the American pragmatist tradition of
thought, see Bloom, *Agon*, pp. 38–41.

means necessary to do criticism at all. They fail to realize, in other words, that the primary function of critical theory is not to make the theorist king of the hill but to submit to others for evaluation models for doing criticism. The questions of intention and meaning, of knowledge and belief, do not center around the possibility of apocalyptically envisioning an absolute vantage point separated from critical practice. The critical theorist need not aspire to become the pope, nor need he be seen as the Antichrist. Theorists' models are always experimental, "proved," if that is the right word, by the fact that they aid in getting certain kinds of intellectual work done. (And only some form of "truth" or effective knowledge can ever provide such aid.)[16] While we may want to quarrel with a particular model, as long as we are engaged in teaching students how to read and understand texts, then we must provide them with models of critical activity that they can assimilate and learn to execute successfully, with the ultimate sign of success being, of course, the student's production of his or her own more workable model. At the very least, we must provide students with a style of intellectual production that they can admire and find morally satisfying.

The question, however, is not primarily one of educational self-interest—that to stay in the big business of higher education we need to do certain things to maximize our position vis-à-vis the sciences. Rather, the question is more broadly educational. Given that we have a certain number of students who are still committed to the study of literature and its relations to the entire range of cultural production, how do we meet our responsibilities to service their needs and to reinforce that commitment? Do we attempt, in short, to preserve, develop, and enlarge their access to all the means whereby they can express and establish themselves as critical thinkers in their chosen vocation? Or do we allow the nihilistic implications of theory to combine with the economic fiats coming from Washington, the various state capitals, and college administration offices to destroy the profession by reducing the study of literature to an adjunct of the teaching of composition? Shouldn't we try to defend the profession or, if not, propose viable alternatives to it? It is all too easy today to succumb to cynicism and despair or, worst of all, to become reconciled to the silly spectacle of professional opportunists, old and young alike, anxious for their careers, perpetually jockeying for position, just like a bunch of drones buzzing around their one and only queen.

3

What, then, should the critic do? What is the critic's role? What ought it to be? What can it be? To begin to answer such questions, I want

16. That this notion betrays a lingering realist theory of truth I freely confess.

to examine now the interpretive practices of two of our most influential critics, Emerson and Frye. By focusing on these figures from the distant and the more recent past, I hope to abstract from the rhetorical strategies in two of their central works those underlying principles of critical activity which may provide us with the basis for a viable model of doing criticism that we can learn to practice for our own collective benefit. My project, then, would be an example of "monumental history" in Nietzsche's sense of the term in "Of the Advantage and Disadvantage of History for Life." I turn to the past not to find some all-determining overview but rather to recover from other bad times inspiring possibilities of imaginative survival that may be applicable in this time of revisionary nightmares.

The two works by Emerson and Frye are "The Divinity School Address" (1838) and "The Imaginative and the Imaginary" (1962). Both are lectures, given from generally unconventional points of view to potentially hostile audiences composed almost entirely of experts on the topics. Emerson and Frye both attempt to distinguish the principle of authentic creativity in religion and in literature from the degraded conventional forms available in their cultures. And both attempt to convert their audiences to their points of view. To this end, they argue synoptically, ranging widely over the entire sweep of religious and cultural history for their examples, and conclude their performances on an emotional, even prophetic note, as they defend the freely creating mind against the enormous pressures of society, in a valiant attempt to make possible a more enlightened, free, and humane future. In other words, they embrace the dialectic of revisionism, refuse to remain stuck in its reductive phase, and attempt to turn it to their own visionary purposes, against the background of darkening hopes in the times that saw, respectively, the beginnings of the Mexican War and the debacle in Vietnam.

The differences between the pieces are of no less interest. Emerson, of course, eschews all mediating structures standing between the individual soul and its visionary prospects as he separates the true religion of moral sentiment from its fallen embodiments in historical creeds, including that of Christianity. In trying to convert his audience of newly ordained Unitarian ministers to his "doctrine of the soul," Emerson condemns as preposterous impositions all the dogmas, rites, and traditional practices to which these young ministers plan to devote their lives. For Emerson, such degraded and degrading forms encourage a self-defeating imitation of outworn practices. For this reason he admonishes his audience, in a more radical fashion than even his heirs Knapp and Michaels do, "to go alone; to refuse the good models. . . . Imitation cannot go above its model. The imitator dooms himself to hopeless mediocrity. The inventor did it because it was natural to him, and so in him it has a charm. In the imitator something else is natural, and he bereaves himself of his own beauty, to come short of another man's."[17] Following from this radical advice ("dare to love God," he also enjoins us, "without mediator or veil"), Emerson concludes that not even a new religion can be efficacious, since one cult more or less makes little difference (p. 81). All cults are gratuitous obstacles to the freely creating soul, that genius of the race that acts through the genius of individual men. Only the new Teacher of the venerable but always fresh doctrine of the soul can make a real difference. For only such a Teacher will be able to unite in his visionary oracles the various fragments of the religious and scientific cultures of Emerson's time:

> The question returns, What shall we do?
>
> I look for the hour when that supreme Beauty which ravished the souls of those Eastern men, and chiefly of those Hebrews, and through their lips spoke oracles to all time, shall speak in the West also. . . . I look for the new Teacher that shall follow so far those shining laws that he shall see them come full circle; shall see their rounding complete grace; shall see the world to be the mirror of the soul; shall see the identity of the law of gravitation with purity of heart; and shall show that the Ought, that Duty, is one thing with Science, with Beauty, and with Joy. [Pp. 82, 84]

Emerson would thus complete and make whole the fragmentary oracles of past beauty by replacing the educational apparatuses of American institutions with this immediate vision of spiritual reality, a vision which the inspiring presence of the prophetic Teacher, who glows with truth, will represent in the minds of his auditors.

Frye, on the other hand, not only concedes to his psychiatric audience an important mediating role (they help the suffering individual adjust to the harsh realities of social life), but he assumes that all institutional operatives should ideally stand in a similar position. Unlike Emerson, who proposes his antinomian, radically revisionary doctrine of the freely creating soul, Frye barely sketches in but nonetheless heavily relies on the solid "doctrinal" basis of his theoretical system as adumbrated in the *Anatomy of Criticism* (1957). In fact, as he traces the development of Renaissance literary notions of melancholy and mania to the psychoanalytic complexes of anxiety neurosis and mass hysteria, one observes how his own essay repeats in miniature the major visionary theme and form of the larger, genially satiric work. Finally, Frye turns not to the idea of a prophetic educator who will radiate a new vision of health and spiritual freedom but to the implicitly moral visions embedded in two canonical texts, *Don Quixote* and *The Prelude,* visions so subtle

17. Ralph Waldo Emerson, *The Selected Writings,* ed. Brooks Atkinson (New York, 1968), p. 81; all further references to this work will be included in the text.

and refined that only the discerning if self-effacing literary critic can make them manifest to others, thanks to his powerful historical memory. The critic is able to discern and then teach others to discern "the solid core of moral reality in the middle of [Don Quixote's] fantasy that holds the loyalty not only of Sancho but of the readers of his adventures."[18] Thus, the critic enables us to recover "the child's vision" of "a golden age," "something that makes Quixotes of us all, and gives our minds, too, whatever dignity they may possess" (p. 165). Similarly, it is the critic in Wordsworth that can read in his dream of the "semi-Quixote," who flees from "some unimaginable catastrophe" while carrying a stone and a shell that are also books representative of words and numbers, a parable of the plight facing any imaginative person living in apocalyptic times. Wordsworth's semi-Quixote bears the emblems of "the two great instruments that man has invented for transforming reality" (p. 166). That is, the critic, like the fictional visionary, must seek to preserve human culture, no matter what the odds.

Frye concludes his lecture by endorsing and updating Wordsworth's remarkable vision of the semi-Quixote in order to win over his audience of tough-minded psychiatrists. First, Frye quotes Wordsworth as the latter testifies to having realized how much akin to this Don Quixote figure he actually is, how fully he identifies with "a Being thus employ'd." Wordsworth goes on to say that given a similar intimation of apocalypse he could go upon "like errand," leaving all else behind and come to share completely in "that maniac's anxiousness." Second, Frye rounds out his elucidating commentary on the apparently apocalyptic vagaries of the visionary imagination by revising Wordsworth and Cervantes and making them appropriate for our time: "Perhaps in the age of the useless bomb-shelter it may be easier for us than it was even for Wordsworth to understand that if the human race is to have any future at all, it can only obtain it through a concern for preserving its powers of creation which it will be difficult, if not impossible, to distinguish clearly from a 'Maniac's anxiousness' " (pp. 165–66). Subtly, carefully, Frye insinuates into the mind of his audience this possible distinction between the authentically creative visions of the truly imaginative creator and the anxiety-ridden phantasmagoria of the neurotic, only to end up suggesting that, given such an age as ours, so literally apocalyptic, this distinction, so important to preserve, may turn out to be moot, as the visions of the creator and the nightmares of the madman come to seem, to neither's benefit, in the glittering shadow of the mushroom cloud, identically eerie.[19]

The differences between Emerson and Frye could not be any more striking than in their conclusions. Emerson stands proudly at the begin-

18. Northrop Frye, "The Imaginative and the Imaginary," *Fables of Identity* (New York, 1963), p. 165; all further references to this work will be included in the text.
19. Frye, of course, not only "lowers" vision to the position of madness here, he also "raises" the torments of the madman to the heights of vision—or at the least leaves the question in suspense.

ning of the historical processes which formed the institution of literary study, and he freely projects his prophetic image of the Teacher to come, the Messiah figure to whom he sees himself as precursor.[20] This quite open self-portrayal accounts for the self-conscious circular structure of his talk. For what at the end of the lecture he predicts for the Teacher, he himself has already partially fulfilled in his rhapsodic, biblical-sounding opening:

> In this refulgent summer, it has been a luxury to draw the breath of life. The grass grows, the buds burst, the meadow is spotted with fire and gold in the tint of flowers. The air is full of birds, and sweet with the breath of the pine, the balm-of-Gilead, and the new hay. Night brings no gloom to the heart with its welcome shade. Through the transparent darkness the stars pour their almost spiritual rays. Man under them seems a young child, and his huge globe a toy. . . . One is constrained to respect the perfection of this world in which our senses converse. How wide; how rich; what invitation from every property it gives to every faculty of man! . . . it is well worth the pith and heart of great men to subdue and enjoy it. The planters, the mechanics, the inventors, the astronomers, the builders of cities, and the captains, history delights to honor. [P. 67]

Clearly, Emerson is doing here what he calls for at the end of his talk and creating a vision, apparently like that of the Hebrew prophets, which, in uniting the laws of the spirit with those of matter, goes much further than any biblical precedent. In short, Emerson structures his performance as a self-fulfilling prophecy by playing Christ to his own John the Baptist.[21]

Everything crucial about Emerson's lecture is in the Protestant, Romantic, visionary tradition; and everything crucial about Frye's lecture fits the Anglo-Catholic, commonsensical, modernist tradition of criticism.[22] Whereas Emerson not only sounds like a prophet and projects himself as the precursor of the new, strangely sensual, and materialistic Messiah to come, Frye not only sounds like a professional academic but projects himself as the Sancho Panza–like appreciator (rather than denigrator) of all the semi-Quixotes in our Western literary tradition:

> In Part Two of the book, Quixote and Sancho come into the dominions of a duke who has read Part One, and who, to amuse

20. The materialistic and imperialistic overtones of this entire passage are quite striking. Space prohibits, however, further discussion.
21. That Walt Whitman came along to interrupt this romance of interpretation is one of those accidents of literary history that one must be grateful for.
22. Totalizer that Frye is, it is not surprising that he should work within the reserved, neoclassical prose idiom of Samuel Johnson, Matthew Arnold, and T. S. Eliot in order to revive the Romantic tradition.

himself, makes Sancho the governor of an island. We are perhaps less surprised than he to learn that Sancho rules his island so honestly and efficiently that he has to be pulled out of office in a hurry before he starts to disintegrate the Spanish aristocracy. We are even less surprised to find that Quixote's advice to him is full of gentle and shrewd good sense. The world is still looking for that lost island, and it still asks for nothing better than to have Sancho Panza for its ruler and Don Quixote for his honoured counsellor. [Pp. 165–66]

If Frye in his more genial manner would play, as do Knapp and Michaels in their reductive fashion, Sancho Panza to all our quixotic visionaries, he must know that he appears to his audience of plain honest men like the "honoured counsellor" in his reading of *Don Quixote.* Frye's sense of his possible self-images and of his audience's possible self-recognitions is every bit as powerful and acute as Emerson's, only in a different register—that of critical irony rather than that of the critical sublime. Such self-conscious art unites Emerson and Frye, despite the differences previously underlined.

In fact these works now begin to resemble each other again. When Emerson adopts the prophetic mode and strikes the heroic stance as he points to the early version of the central man trope, he stresses how this new Teacher is to be incarnated in his own texts by means of the self-fulfilling circular structure of his talk. Similarly Frye, although he adopts the plain-speaking mode and strikes an ironic posture, also points to a great facilitator of the moral vision now implicit in literary texts—that reflexive critic who is cut, subliminally at least, in the minds of his auditors as they attempt to follow his authoritative citations and interpretations of texts not immediately available to everyone's memory. My point is not, however, that Emerson and Frye are the same and that both of them are touched in the head because, à la Knapp and Michaels, they set themselves up as hermeneutic gods; nor is it that Frye fulfills Emerson's prophecy of the new Teacher and Knapp and Michaels fulfill Frye's worst fears concerning a "Maniac's anxiousness"; rather, what I hope to suggest by comparing Emerson and Frye is that some experimental, yes, even "theoretical," generalizations about their practices can be made, generalizations that could suggest the outlines of a model of doing criticism that one could characterize—good heavens!—as rational and affirmative.

4

But can one really abstract common critical principles from these related but also very different works? Naturally, I believe that one can.

As far as I can see, there are six such principles of critical activity.[23] I term the first one "the principle of opposition." Whatever the religious, political, or aesthetic ideology of the critic, he should strive to maintain an oppositional stance vis-à-vis the dominant conventions in his discipline and, more generally, in his society. This principle should not be implemented blindly, of course, nor in a reflexlike manner. The critic's opposition must arise from the particular situation of the profession. Consider, for example, how Emerson confronts directly the bankruptcy of the clerisy with his doctrine of the freely creating soul, a prophetic provocation, as it were. Or take Frye. He patiently and wittily traces the origins of psychoanalysis back to its roots in the literary imagination and so disarms in advance the audience's potential critique of literature. In both cases the critic opposes the specter of historical or psychological determinism in behalf of the human imagination. Such a stance must continue to be adopted given the various determinisms of the Right and the Left, of the old guard and the deconstructive cutting edge.

My second principle is that of "accommodation." It follows naturally from the first. It requires the critic, in turning to past or future for inspiration, to address directly and honestly, without the coy evasions of self-conscious irony, the intellectual needs of the interpretive community. Frye, for instance, gives his lecture in 1962 amidst the bomb-shelter craze, a time that saw not only the beginnings of American escalation in Vietnam but, as well, the Cuban missile crisis. This background explains, in part, Frye's manner of updating the moral vision embedded in the texts of Wordsworth and Cervantes.[24] Frye accommodates the vision of these texts and the situation of his time to one other. Similarly, Emerson enunciates his "doctrine of the soul"—that there are immutable spiritual laws arising out of man's moral nature that can make prophets of us all—in order to rouse his audience from its dogmatic or cynical slumber. Thus, the principle of accommodation means more than just topicality. It means, as well, that the critic must attempt to comprehend in as systematic a fashion as possible the relationship between his profession and the needs of the community at large, a task that one could argue defines the theoretical enterprise Knapp and Michaels want to bring to an end.

The third principle is "the principle of judgment." However difficult it may seem today to draw any hard-and-fast distinctions between the authentically creative imagination and the merely conventional, degraded, or empty form, the critic must make the attempt, especially if he is going to ask others to devote their lives to a vocation dedicated to the appreciation and analysis of cultural productions. If the

23. That Bloom's revisionary ratios also total six in number is, I believe, no accident.
24. I prefer to use the weak term "updating" instead of "revising" because what is involved is not a willful misreading and distortion of the text but the use of the inherent semantic indeterminacy (usually, quite limited) of any text for topical purposes.

last principle is crucial to the theoretical enterprise, then this one is crucial to the practice of criticism. Even Emerson, for all his anti-nomianism, does not ask his audience to abandon Christianity in despair or to found a new religion. Rather he enjoins them to infuse the old forms with the new spirit of his doctrine of the soul. Similarly, although Frye claims that it may become increasingly difficult to distinguish a maniac's anxiousness from creative energy, he does not propose to stop trying to do so, as the title of his piece indicates.

The fourth principle, that of "programmatic action," means that whether the critic points to the living examples of particular individuals or holds up models of a critical system, he ought to propose some program of intellectual activity, no matter how experimental, provisional, or revisionary. This principle is obviously the hardest to define to everyone's satisfaction. But given the examples of Emerson and Frye, let me attempt to speculate on some practical suggestions. Both Emerson and Frye in their talks provide occasions for what in "Spiritual Laws" Emerson calls our moments of "revisal" or "correction." These are "epochs of our life" in which "a silent thought by the wayside as we walk . . . revises our entire manner of life and says—'Thus hast thou done, but it were better thus' " (p. 206). In other words, Emerson and Frye act on our imagination in a way that calls us to judgment. They suggest why we must convert to a faith in the creative power of the human imagination. Whether or not we can summon up the will for such a faith is an open question.

The fifth principle, that of "formal self-effacement," means that no matter how obviously or subtly one presents oneself as either a cultural Messiah or a plain honest man ("one of us"), the critic should subordinate the impulse to promote himself to the larger communicable vision he is proposing for critical evaluation. On the face of it, this principle would seem to be the one that needs little or no comment. We all detest the critic who encourages a cult of personality to spring up around him, no matter what kind of cult or personality may be involved. Both the later Eliot's studied modesty and Bloom's chronic afflatus often detract from the fine points they would make.[25] Neither Emerson nor Frye, despite their self-projections, seems like either the sly priest with an insidious doctrine to insinuate or the great man with the big voice. However one sees their textual identities, Emerson and Frye put themselves forward as heralds of a positive vision of spiritual laws and imaginative creation. They are trying to articulate a vision for their particular communities. Their styles, which facilitate rather than frustrate communication, testify to this motivation. But their representative status

---

25. Clearly I recognize the powerful self-projections in both Emerson and Frye. However, such self-displays do not appear to be the primary motivating factor.

does not depend solely on the authority of their styles. Rather it depends as much, perhaps more, on the quality and care that their styles reveal. Finally, the sixth principle is that of "self-revision." However un-propitious the times, however alike he makes critical idealism and critical nihilism seem, the critic should try to ground the education of his students on a heuristic or regulative ideal of critical activity that can lead them out of their apprenticeship to any particular system or methodology into their scholarly maturity so they may become the originators of their own stances and accommodating theories.[26] Recall Emerson and Frye once again. They do not turn against the soul or the imagination, nor even against the ministry or the profession of psychiatry, simply because the age seems to demand an ironic image of its accelerated grimace. Instead they critique the present decadence in the name of an intentionally open-ended, admittedly prophetic vision of human potential, a vision clearly derived from the cultural past. That is, they too practice monumental history in Nietzsche's sense and take the risk that their "modest proposals" *for* something might also make them seem eligible, in some people's eyes, for the madhouse.

I offer these six principles in barest outline. I do so not simply for provocation's sake. The profession is in horrible shape, and we must begin addressing the situation seriously. If you were a graduate student now and had just finished reading "Against Theory," would you willingly choose to belong to a profession that appears to be openly and irremediably nihilistic? Whoever *did* enter the profession would help to turn it into a haven for the hopelessly neurotic, at best, or, at worst, an asylum for the purely pathological. And unless one has some perverse, self-destructive need to play (whether intentionally or not) Sancho Panza to one's own Don Quixote, or Emerson of "Experience" to Emerson of "Self-Reliance," or even Knapp and Michaels to their own Fish, the question of the function of criticism at the present time demands to be treated and not left to the sublime cynicism of Schopenhauer or any of his belated avatars: "The mind, tormented so greatly, destroys, as it were, the thread of its memory, fills up the gaps with fictions, and thus seeks refuge in madness from the mental suffering that exceeds its strength, just as a limb affected by mortification is cut off and replaced with a wooden one."[27] Could it be, I wonder, as Schopenhauer's remarks ironically suggest, that what, for the sake of argument, one can fairly characterize as revisionary madness could also be seen as an uncanny

26. With this latter qualification, I believe that I avoid the risk of simply repeating the revisionary pattern previously discussed, at least as it works itself out in such essays as "Against Theory." Without offering a vision of their own to replace theory, Knapp and Michaels can more easily be assimilated by the old guard, who do have a certain vision of what the future of literary criticism and theory should be.
27. Schopenhauer, *The World as Will and Representation*, 1:193.

restoration to health? Could it be that our profession had to go through its deconstructive phase in order to begin over again, what was apparently lost in New Critical method having been supplemented by even more powerful interpretive techniques grafted from continental sources? Would this mean that the critic best embodies Freud's image from *Civilization and Its Discontents* of man as a prosthetic god? Or does this mean only that the would-be revisionist who entertains such a vision is possessed by a "gaiety transfiguring all that dread," because he may soon become as plainly mad as the next university don?[28]

28. W. B. Yeats, "Lapis Lazuli," *The Collected Poems* (New York, 1956), p. 292.

Against Theory?

E. D. Hirsch, Jr.

I agree with a lot of the theories in "Against Theory" by Steven Knapp and Walter Benn Michaels. I see their essay as expressing some of my own oft-stated objections to the pretensions of literary theory and critical method, though Knapp and Michaels imply that it's *my* theory they are arguing against. But on the very first page of *Validity in Interpretation* (1967) I wrote: "No methods of legal, biblical, or literary construction have ever been devised which are not in some instances either misleading or useless."[1] And in a 1982 issue of *Critical Inquiry* I was still repeating my objections to the pretensions of literary theory when it tries to dictate the forms of critical practice.[2] When Knapp and Michaels make similar objections, my instinct is to welcome two forceful writers to the ranks of the antitheoretical theorists. (May their numbers increase!) But I'm sorry that when they turned to the subject of intention they found it useful to turn me into a straw man. Too bad. We antitheorists should stick together. In this brief rejoinder I want to state my intentionalist argument (or rather "the" intentionalist argument, for P. F. Strawson and others have used it) in what I consider to be its accurate form. Then I shall challenge one or two points in the Knapp-Michaels exposition.

It isn't accurate to suggest that before Knapp and Michaels came along intentionalists imagined "a moment of interpretation before intention is present" (p. 14). Knapp and Michaels are certainly right to reject that idea. And the intentionalist argument rejects it too. It holds

1. E. D. Hirsch, Jr., *Validity in Interpretation* (New Haven, Conn., 1967), p. vii.
2. See my "The Politics of Theories of Interpretation," *Critical Inquiry* 9 (Sept. 1982): 235–47.

Reprinted from the June 1983 issue of *Critical Inquiry*.

that intention is formally necessary at every moment of interpretation and that there can be no construed meaning without intention. One basis for this claim of formal necessity is as follows: all sequences of phonemes or graphemes can sustain more than one type of construed meaning. For instance, they might sustain allusive or nonallusive, ironical or nonironical, literal or nonliteral construed meanings. But every type of construed meaning is what it is and not some other type of meaning that might have been construed. So terms like "intention," "speech act," and "authorship" are needed to indicate the formally required agency that makes the construed meaning this type rather than that in any instance of interpretation.

That's the core of the intentionalist argument, and versions of it are well stated by Knapp and Michaels. I think they are right to say that there can be no construed meaning without intention, and I particularly like their formulation when they say that "pinning down an interpretation of the sentence will not involve adding a speaker but deciding among a range of possible speakers" (p. 14). But in this formulation Knapp and Michaels believe themselves to be stating a view that is at odds with my own. I wish to assure them that they are not. For I am not now nor have I ever been a proponent of "a moment of interpretation before intention is present." I emphatically agree with their statement that phonemes and graphemes "become signifiers only when they acquire meanings, and when they lose their meanings they stop being signifiers" (p. 23).

Having now incinerated Hirsch the straw man and replaced him with somebody who also rejects the idea of pre-intentional construed language, I still find some points to disagree with in Knapp and Michaels' argument. I just don't see the consequentiality of their argument at its most novel and crucial point—which I take to be their assertion about the practical nullity of the idea of intention. They reach this conclusion in the following comment on their previous exposition: "We have argued that what a text means and what its author intends it to mean are identical and that their identity robs intention of any theoretical interest" (p. 19). That is to say, since authorial intention is always necessarily being realized in all forms of critical practice, intention can be disregarded as an idea that practice needs to pay any attention to.

What has happened in this inference seems to me a case of what Henry Sams used to call "semantic slippage." Up to this point, Knapp

---

E. D. Hirsch, Jr., professor of English at the University of Virginia, is the author of numerous works, including *Validity in Interpretation* and *The Aims of Interpretation*.

50 E. D. Hirsch, Jr.

and Michaels had argued that a text's meaning, being intentional, must always be what *an* author intends it to mean. They now say that a text's meaning must always be what *its* author intends it to mean. That switch would be consequent only if "its author" is taken to mean something special like "the author of whatever meanings are being construed from the text." But the inference would not be consequent if we take "its author" in its usual sense of "the composer of the text." Text-authorship and meaning-authorship are not the same. Moreover, there's a more serious semantic slippage with respect to meaning-authorship itself. Suppose we understand Knapp and Michaels to use the phrase "the intentions of its author" in the normal way to imply the meanings that *had been* intended by the composer of the text in composing it. That would raise problems for their identity thesis. As I tried to explain to Knapp and Michaels in a conversation at Berkeley about a year ago, "what the author intended" and "what the author intends" do not necessarily amount to the same thing. The past tense could refer to a past meaning-event, the present tense to a current and different type of meaning-event. Introducing the idea of history, of pastness, would give the Knapp-Michaels thesis a rather different twist, as in the following reformulation: we have argued that what a text now means and what its author intended it to mean are identical. So long as we stick to the present tense, we are justified only in saying that "what a text now means is what some postulated author is intending it to mean"—a singularly uninteresting observation.

Why did Knapp and Michaels commit such an obvious logical misdemeanor? Certainly not because they are oblivious to logical cogency but probably because they think there is no pragmatic difference between "what an author intends" and "what an author intended." They probably think that in practice what an author intended *is* what the current reader believes that the author intended. Isn't that the sort of point they are making in their discussion of "true belief" on pages 27–29? In their view, our current belief about the author's past intention is the only intention we have. Thus "intends" and "intended" are for practical purposes the same.

But hold on a minute. Even granting, for the sake of argument, the equation of belief and knowledge, still "intends" and "intended" would be the same only if we *believed* we were construing what the author intended. But some critics don't believe they are doing that. For them, belief about what "an" author intends and about what the composer of the text intended are not the same. Even under the pragmatic equation of belief and knowledge "intends" and "intended" are here different. But just at this point Knapp and Michaels seem to relinquish the idea that true belief is knowledge. They say that when Paul de Man or some other critic truly believes his interpretation of a text is not what its author intended, that critic is just making an ontological mistake. He is trying "to separate things that should not be separated: on the ontological side, meaning from intention, . . . on the epistemological side, knowledge from true belief." These "separated terms are *in fact* inseparable" (p. 29; italics mine). So even if we think we are separating the meaning of a text from what its author intended, we are in fact making a mistake. We always do understand what its author intended. This seems to be "in fact" an empirical claim.

But there is precious little empirical evidence to support such a strong and universalistic empirical claim. Take this example. When Blake re-authored his 1789 *Songs of Innocence* in 1794, he didn't change the texts of the poems at all. But his second interpretation was not the same as "what the author intended" in his first interpretation. In 1794 Blake believes that what he now intends is not what he then intended in 1789 by his text. Is he just stating a "preference" that is "irrelevant to the theory of interpretation" (p. 18 n.7)? Is he committing the ontological mistake of imagining a pre-intentional language? As far as I can see, neither ontology nor fact support the identification of "intends" and "intended." We do not always understand by a text what we believe its author meant in composing it. The empirical claim of Knapp and Michaels seems to be false.

* * *

When I first started writing about intention in the 1950s, one of my aims was to resist the then current pretensions of literary theory in telling critical practice what it ought to do. The New Critical doctrine which says that it isn't legitimate or possible to consider intention was a rhetorical instrument designed to discourage some critical practices and encourage others. My purpose in resisting this rhetorical use of theory was to liberate critics to deal with all taboo problems that seemed interesting or valuable—including problems of original intention. Knapp and Michaels, despite their antitheoretical disclaimers, seem, like New Critics before them, to want to banish explicit considerations of original intention from critical practice. In this they are as "theoretical" as W. K. Wimsatt or René Wellek, and their theory amounts in practice to straight New Criticism. Knapp and Michaels suggest that there's no point in self-consciously trying to discover an author's intention because we are always already doing so. All the to-do about finding the author's original intention "creates the illusion of a choice between alternative methods of interpreting" (p. 18). But there is no choice. The author's intention is already present in every construing.

What is the practical effect of this "antitheoretical" principle? The most probable effect is to foster the comforting idea that there's no point in pursuing historical scholarship. We are always already doing so. Maybe that effect on practice isn't what Knapp and Michaels intended.

Nonetheless, their argument can readily be taken as a sanction for historically ignorant practice, on the grounds that historical ignorance is really an "illusion." We always do construe what the author means (meant).

One of the best uses of literary theory is to innoculate students against the purely rhetorical influences of theory upon practice, whether that rhetoric is theoretical or antitheoretical. The usual mark of a purely rhetorical use of theory is some ontological claim that we do not "really" have the choices we think we have. My counterclaim is that critical practice is what we choose to make it. Meaning is a stipulative not an ontological entity. It too is what we choose to make it. I prefer this anti-ontological argument against theory to the ontological antitheory of Knapp and Michaels. I'll repeat that argument as I made it in 1967, and with the same intentions: "Any normative concept in interpretation implies a choice that is required not by the nature of written texts but rather by the goal that the interpreter sets himself. It is a weakness in many descriptions of the interpretive process that this act of choice is disregarded and the process described as though the object of interpretation were somehow determined by the ontological status of texts themselves."[3]

3. Hirsch, *Validity*, p. 24.

Toward Uncritical Practice

Jonathan Crewe

In their essay "Against Theory," Steven Knapp and Walter Benn Michaels challenge in the most uncompromising terms the value and even the bare possibility of "doing theory." Given the present sanctified status of theory one can appreciate the authors' iconoclastic impulse, but their discussion remains provocative in ways that call for a response. If I were to take it seriously enough (and the authors leave room for suspicion that they are in earnest), the antitheoretical position would entail a significant, and in my view retrogressive, change in professional attitude.

Before elaborating on this charge I must acknowledge that the authors attempt an antitheoretical *argument*. It is one that in essence denies an ability to establish any (logical?) vantage point prior to, or superior to, practice, and hence denies an ability ever to determine, from an extra-practical standpoint, any fundamental principle capable of founding or rationalizing interpretation. Practice, we are told, is always institutionally or otherwise given, always encompasses us, and belated attempts to seize control in the name of principle are consequently foredoomed. "Doing" theory accordingly becomes a mode of impotent presumption equivalent to doing nothing, while the theoretical impulse represents nothing more than a desire to escape from practice. (In the zero-sum world of these authors, theory always "loses"—has always already lost—what practice "wins.")

Such in outline is the argument against theory, one that depends on a particular understanding of the nature and limits of theory but even more on an assumption of the inviolable (if unrecognized) sovereignty of practice. By implication practice *contains* and legitimizes all the theory it

Reprinted from the June 1983 issue of *Critical Inquiry*.

ever needs, making any further theory, or independent theoretical principle, superfluous. Practice thus becomes self-sufficient and all-encompassing, while any opposition to it, whether formal or actual, is vain.

Although I will have to look more closely at this argument in order to assess it, one can already anticipate its effect of exalting practice. But since this promotion is unaccompanied by any further account of practice (Do we all know what practice entails?), one may also recognize that manipulation of the terms "theory" and "practice" may result in a forensic triumph for the latter. This is indeed the hollow victory for which I see the authors contending, but it should not be assumed on that account that nothing is really at stake in the attempt.[1] Not only are the authors' own terms revealing when we examine them, but there is more to being "against theory" than has thus far appeared. The argument I have paraphrased is yoked to an elusive conception of pragmatic interpretation, and it is also made to justify a number of surprising claims about the nature and power of belief.[2] And the exceptional significance of the antitheoretical message is advertised by a rhetoric of unusually high pressure and premature dogmatism. What are we to make of it all?

In my own view the antitheoretical argument (which could rank as a contribution only *in* the field of critical theory, from which it never escapes) is here at the service of an emergent ideology of the interpretive caste or guild, an ideology under which a privileged status quo would be secured against fundamental questioning. My aim will be to suggest what this ideology consists in and also to question the antitheoretical argument used to justify it. I will not, however, feel obliged to defend (perhaps unnecessarily) the theoreticians whose work Knapp and Michaels pronounce "mistaken" or "incoherent," though I will implicitly defend theory. If Knapp and Michaels might say that I have already missed the point—that what they consider failures are not those of named individuals but of any theoretical undertaking at all—I would

1. The authors consistently describe theory as a form of impotent delusion, of error rather than evil. They thus leave unexplained the point of being so vehemently "against theory." What can it possibly matter?
2. The authors might reasonably claim that pragmatism is being thrust upon them, since that is not how they choose to characterize themselves. I would welcome any other term they might supply to name their own position, since such a term is "missing" at present.

Jonathan Crewe, assistant professor of English at the Johns Hopkins University, is the author of *Unredeemed Rhetoric: Thomas Nashe and the Scandal of Authorship.* He has recently completed work on sixteenth-century literature of the monstrous and the prodigious and is currently engaged in a full-length study of the politics of Renaissance comedy.

reply that they draw the wrong conclusions from their evidence and, indeed, exploit that evidence to uphold a prejudicial characterization of theory. Insofar as they consider failure *inevitable* on the theoretical plane, they are themselves forced to settle not for a properly emancipated practice but for an attitude of precritical primitivism. Thus what might seem, given the history of the profession during the past two decades, like a timely move beyond theory turns out in fact to be a return to a condition "before" theory.

For the particulars let us turn to what is actually said in "Against Theory":

> By "theory" we mean a special project in literary criticism: the attempt to govern interpretations of particular texts by appealing to an account of interpretation in general. [P. 11]

It is not clear at once if all or only some of "theory" as generally understood is included here, nor is it clear what "a special project" refers to. We are, however, offered some help in the next sentence: "literary subjects [*sic*] with no direct [?] bearing on the interpretation of individual works, such as narratology, stylistics, and prosody" are excluded. But since these exclusions are also designated "empirical" (i.e., nontheoretical anyway?), the value of the clarification is doubtful. How much of currently recognized theory is "inside" practice and how much is extrapractical assumption? We will never know.

What we are left with, however, is a definition of theory ("doing" theory) that significantly excludes any reference to processes or conditions under which "an account of interpretation in general" might be formulated, desired, or derived from practice. Doing theory thus excludes what might normally be considered definitive concerns of the theorist, while theory itself is taken preemptively to be an illegitimate imposition *on* practice, never a term dialectically paired with practice or the product of a theoretical moment that need not forever preclude the moment of practice. The prescriptive nature and motivation of theory is seemingly taken for granted as is the passive-restrictive attitude of the theorist.

In view of all this we might assume that the authors are indeed confronting a special and perhaps illegitimate case of theory—that that is what "a special project" means—but their refusal to qualify the general term or to exclude anything explicitly means that more can always be understood (or intended) than the limited case. It is hard to believe that this is an accident. The impression prevails that theory itself is on the line, and the issue is not resolved either way once Knapp and Michaels begin to deal with particular cases. In the act of defining their own terms, moreover, Knapp and Michaels present something like an already deconstructed or unmasked version of theory, one that purports to show theory for what it is as a tool of institutional domination. Doing theory involves nothing more than trying to *govern* (illegitimately control?) practical interpretation by *appealing* (passively, improperly?) to a source of authority as given. The nullity or arbitrariness of the source is presupposed in the terms of the definition, as a result of which the question of *theory* is in a sense begged throughout the essay. Although Knapp and Michaels later try to account (with what degree of plausibility we will see) for the genesis of theory, is the a priori nature of the beast that is insinuated in the opening definition, remaining to color all their conceptions? (It should not be supposed, however, that opposition to the dominating effects, or at least pretensions, of theory promises any emancipation from such effects, which will be relocated in practice.)

A certain latitude and infelicity—a cavalier treatment of logical and semantic distinctions—mark the antitheoretical argument as it unfolds:

> Some theorists have sought to ground the reading of literary texts in methods designed to guarantee the objectivity and validity of interpretations. [P. 11]

If some theorists *have* done this, it is also true that grounding interpretations in "methods" constitutes an activity of a different order from that of appealing to a general account. The effect of the statement, introduced without any explanatory transition, is thus to broaden the scope of theory, at the same time bringing a second order of grounding and perhaps a second class of offenders under suspicion. Moreover, distinctions that may not be commensurate and generate radically different kinds of discourse cease to count from the standpoint of pure practice, the flattening reductiveness of which appears in the equivalent treatment of such terms as "valid" and "objective," or "valid interpretation" and "meaning."[3] (It might seem carping to mention this if it did not anticipate the systematic denial of logical and semantic distinctions that later emerges as the grand principle on which the authors proceed.)

There is more to come:

> Others, impressed by the inability of such procedures to produce agreement [about valid interpretation] have translated that failure into an alternative mode of theory that denies the possibility of correct interpretation. [P. 11]

Does the original definition of theory still hold, since it seems that it must now include the *derivation* of a new principle from failures in practice? And can it accommodate the apparent shift from an attempt to govern

---

3. The authors might suggest that they merely reproduce the usage of those they oppose, yet they fail effectively to distinguish where reporting ends and their own terminology begins.

practice to the practical discovery, subsequently formalized, that that interpretation is ungovernable? Is the *denial* of any single correct interpretation equivalent to governing interpretation? And is the original definition still being unpacked or (again?) rewritten when we are told that:

> Theory attempts to solve—or celebrate the impossibility of solving—a set of familiar problems: the function [?] of authorial intention, the status of literary language, the role of interpretive assumptions, and so on. [P. 11]

As defined, theory does not attempt to solve these problems or ones like them but rather appeals to a general account under which heterogeneous problems of this order either cease to be problems or are solved preemptively, at least in principle. And if that is what the authors "obviously" meant anyway, will we have to regard the nature and motivation of theory somewhat differently, recognizing in it a principle of interpretive economy?

The point to be made here is not just that Knapp and Michaels assail theory—to which they are entitled—but rather that a leapfrogging imprecision and facility in their characterization of theory call for resistance. The theory they oppose is theory superficially characterized, stripped down to stark alternatives, and denied its own claims, while the opposition is conducted in a style of sweeping incrimination that does not condescend to pause over details. If theory "loses," it is hardly surprising under the circumstances.

The next phase of the argument against theory, like all succeeding phases, is greatly facilitated by the trojan-horse definition with which the essay begins: concede *that* and everything else falls into place. But without succumbing to this preparation, let us consider the alleged origin of theory in error, an origin that virtually constitutes "theory" as "error" and vice versa. The "mistake" theorists always make, we are told, but which also remains the sole enabling condition of theory, is to divide what is in reality indivisible. Theorists always fail to recognize "the fundamental inseparability of the elements involved" (p. 12). (To the question "Involved in *what?*" the antitheoretical answer, repeated indefinitely, can only be "reality.") So in making a distinction, for example, between the meaning of a text and its authorial intention, theorists divide what is in reality indivisible, whatever "it" may be. They also presumably divide what should be a unified critical discourse by articulating their own arguments on one of the paired terms; thus we may get discursive theorists of intention, instead of practical critics doing what comes naturally.

Having once divorced meaning from intention (to continue with the same example), the theorist can then take the next step, which is to privilege one of the paired terms as a so-called grounding term, to derive from it the second term, and to make the grounding term at once the object of his theory and the source of his control over practice. Thus "intention" may become the grounding term from which "meaning" is derived; if we want to know the meaning of a text we will, as theoretical "intentionalists," proceed to recover an authorial intention in the light of which meaning can be established.

But, say Knapp and Michaels, in reality (i.e., in "always already" on-the-go practice) there is simply no difference between the meaning and the authorial intention of an interpretable text; to "have" one is to "have" the other simultaneously and indistinguishably. To attempt any distinction is "unreal," while to make one term the object of theory is always to have presupposed the other as well, making any procedure of grounding and derivation "incoherent." That is all there is to it.

Setting aside the question of whether there might be a way of doing theory that could acknowledge such difficulties (i.e., a conscious way of doing theory rather than a blindly wilful one), I will suggest only that such antitheoreticalism is an argument of extreme innocence or premature despair. Making distinctions where they do not exist "in reality" may be a condition (it is certainly a recognized risk) of any form of understanding whatever. The alternative, regrettably, is not always a closer lived proximity to the real but more often a blind, ritualistic practice that adheres to a forever mystified first cause. The practice envisaged in "Against Theory" might thus indeed be mysterious, either in the sense that it could be like that of an enthusiastic cult without a formal theology or (more likely) in the sense that it could mean business as usual, a defensive adherence to the procedures and values of the guild (in which case the roles of apprentice and master would exclusively define professional existence).

It apparently does not occur to Knapp and Michaels—at least not with enough force—that to deny distinctions is not *thereby* to reenter in practice the condition of reality, nor does it seemingly occur to them that the existence of logical and semantic distinctions does not necessarily imply a prior undivided substance. Such artificially constructed distinctions may require us to *posit* an undivided entity to which they analytically refer, but to assume that the undoing of distinctions will leave the mind directly in touch with the real stuff is to yield to naive reification or literalism. In collapsing any possible distinction between "intention" and "meaning," for example, Knapp and Michaels may find that they are not left with the reality in which those terms are subsumed and annulled, but with nothing at all—that those distinctions, or ones like them, constitute a reality that may simply disappear as the terms are collapsed. But in fact the authors cannot even do without the terms. While denying E. D. Hirsch and others the right to make distinctions or to advance on a theoretical plane, Knapp and Michaels take advantage of precisely those *existing* distinctions to reaffirm an underlying substance (or immanent textual "presence") on the basis of which practice is licensed to continue.

So the authors have it both ways: they stigmatize distinctions as illusory or "incoherent" but immediately recoup both terms "together" to secure practice. "Doing what we have always done" (we? always? what?) is thus placed beyond doubt and beyond interrogation, becoming a newly entrenched uncritical practice. One might describe as an instance of "bad faith" this maneuver in which the authors disqualify a distinction only to appropriate its effects; the rhetorical ambience in which the maneuver is conducted prompts me however to call it smash and grab, or s. & g. for short.

The frequent recurrence of s. & g. in "Against Theory" shows that the authors simply cannot find a basis on which to *oppose* theory, an authentic opposition demanding a practice of such unprecedented vitality that it "speaks for itself." In reality, the authors stage an opposition that belies a continuing dependence, particularly on the disqualified intentionalism—the terminology and assumptions—of Hirsch. And since the authors are not "free" of theory, their opposition must also entail *correction* of the errors of theory. We will recall that theorists always make two mistakes: that of privileging a grounding term, which itself follows (the authors might say necessarily follows) the first mistake (the authors might almost say original sin) of division. Correction thus requires a reversal of this process of error, which is accomplished once the authors have, so to speak, got two back into one again and the pernicious effects of division have been eliminated.

If antitheoreticians are themselves secure against relapses into error, it is because they respect the power of self-evidence and thus remain the arbiters of reality, not fugitives from it:

> But once it is seen that the meaning of a text is simply identical to the author's intended meaning, the project of *grounding* meaning in intention becomes incoherent. [P. 12]

The illusoriness of the *apparent* division will, in other words, expose itself in the fullness of time ("once") and without any intervention on the part of the observer, who need only stand and wait until "it is seen." What then becomes *self*-evident is that the two terms are actually one ("identical"), after which "they" (or whatever they jointly designate) can continue to dispense "their" beneficial effects. What the authors might say, but do not, is that the discovered "identity" of terms raises questions about logical misconstruction, about the tautologous results of trying to equate "meaning" with "authorial intention," or about the question-begging nature of a particular argument. Their own claims notwithstanding, the authors do not take it that *no* result has been achieved and that the argument has short-circuited but that the *wrong* result has been achieved. All that is needed to rectify matters is a refusal to distinguish at all, a refusal that constitutes the universal nostrum of the pragmatic interpreter.

So much for the theory (supertheory, antitheory) to end all theories. It is a theory that does not presume to alter practice but only to disclose the primordial character and authority of practice, thus defining itself as a petty theodicy of the guild. But since it challenges theory, not only in the name of practice but through a kind of *reductio ad absurdum,* let us turn to the example, destined no doubt to become famous, of the "wave-poem." We will have to recall that the example is offered by its inventors as both a concession and a rebuke to theoretical ways of thinking—as the kind of absurdity that theoretical thinking makes unavoidable—but not as an example called forth by pragmatism. We may however find this example, too, being subjected to s. & g.

We are asked to suppose that while walking along a beach we find the first line of a stanza, "A slumber did my spirit seal," traced in the sand. We naturally suppose that an earlier passerby has traced the words, but then comes a wave that erases the line only to leave in its place the second line of the stanza. It now appears that the wave has *written* the poem by some nonhuman, nonintentional process. Shortly afterward, a submarine surfaces and some dialogue spoken by white-coated figures on board (maybe scientists) indicates that after all a human agency has been responsible for tracing the words; it only seemed that a wave could write the same poem Wordsworth wrote. The point of the example is to make us think, or rather show that we cannot think, of intentionless meaning, which is what we have to attempt while in the grip of a belief that the wave has written the poem. While we believe that the wave is the author of the poem, we can no longer think of it as meaningful; therefore in considering the poem meaningful, as we have always done, we have also always taken for granted its author's intentionality. We cannot even for a moment think of meaning in the absence of intention, which is always (fully?) a co-presence with meaning, therefore any theoretical distinction will be "incoherent." To "have" meaning is identically to "have" intention.

If this example induces a feeling of *déjà vu* rather than illumination, perhaps that is because it is an ornate though significantly weakened version of the familiar example of monkeys on typewriters eventually producing the works of Shakespeare. Let us nevertheless concede the example and see what can be deduced from it. While the example is one that a theorist of any of the schools Knapp and Michaels censure might easily construe in his own favor, it is an example designed to work against theory; we are thus to accept that it "really" shows the flat impossibility of what any theoretician must believe in order to proceed.

Alternatively, it shows the unreality of the situations that theory supposes to be capable of existing. Theory can no more exist in reality than a wave-poem can. (Antitheoreticians inhabit a world of stark realities and unrealities, in which there is no admissible place for fictions, constructive or otherwise.) But now the s. & g. begins: the example *against* theory begins to work *for* pragmatic interpretation. It usefully shows, first of all, what it is both necessary and possible for a pragmatic interpreter to believe in order to sustain his practice; since he, too, would not have been able to interpret the wave-poem, it follows, not that intention is necessary, or that meaning is necessary, but that both are necessary "all at once." The example also usefully enables the authors to determine what the status of a wave-poem would be, supposing that one could be found.

According to the authors the wave inscriptions are uninterpretable in practice because in essence they *are* not words, not sentences, not a poem, not even language. What makes all the difference, restoring interpretability, is the arrival of the submarine with a passenger who can ontologically reconnect those inscriptions to a human-intentional source. But if the wave-inscriptions are practically uninterpretable, what are we to make of them? The safest answer from a pragmatic standpoint might well be nothing. If something has to be said, perhaps that is because the marks are not random or unintelligible; they conform to known rules of syntax, prosody, orthography, and so forth. So Knapp and Michaels do say something. They say that the marks *are* not words, sentences, poetry, language, and so forth but merely *resemble* those things.

To say this is to go overboard for metaphysics in a way that is at least superficially odd in any pragmatic context. It is quite radically to deny that the forms of language possess any defining power; it is also to deny that wherever those forms exist there is inescapably a question of interpretation, even if not an easy one. What normally and irreplaceably defines a sentence, no matter whence it emanates, is a regular grammatical form. Of course this is a matter of convention, in the absence of any "real" definition of a sentence. But to suppose, as the authors evidently do, that the authentic property of the sentence is conferred on it by interpretive belief, irrespective of conventional form, is to be reborn into a condition of "true belief" extreme even in these times for solipsistic intransigence. Alternatively, the supposition that forms are merely empty betrays an obliviousness of the socially constructed and consensual nature of linguistic significance.

Knapp and Michaels, then, *resolve* the status of intentionless inscriptions by introducing with more emphasis than argument the term "resemblance." We are entitled to eject that term as soon as it appears, since in their own example the wave-poem does not *resemble* a poem by Wordsworth but is actually identical to one. What the authors have, whether they like it or not, is a wave-*poem* that happens not to lend itself to pragmatic interpretation; the problem is theirs, but "resemblance" is not the solution. Even to speak of "resemblance" here is to give a wholly arbitrary ontological groundedness to the difference between an interpretable and a noninterpretable text (even when they are the same text); it is also to *secure* interpretation by assuming the power to disqualify (by reduction to its own image or shadow) any poem that fails to meet pragmatic requirements. Unquestionably it is possible to work on such a basis; all that is questionable is the value of doing so.

Since, in the absence of substantial pragmatic argument, not much more can be said about the self-resembling text (the text that is not quite "itself"), let us turn to the question of belief, to which pragmatism attaches great importance. Indeed, the authors might suggest that this is where attention should have been focused all along, since their own investment is in the epistemological rather than the ontological side of the question. Although they are obliged by the perversity of theorists to talk about grounding, that is not a matter with which pragmatism is vitally concerned. Alternatively, their own quasi-grounding is supplied by belief rather than by any inherent property, particular origin, or altogetherness of the text.

True as far as it goes—yet I have tried to show that the ontological grounding of practice is what the authors quietly effect before moving on to the chosen terrain of belief, so by the time they arrive there any problems have been solved in advance. By practicing s. & G. extensively, the authors have reified the object or substance of their belief while at the same time securing that object by placing it beyond analysis. Accordingly no difficulties arise about the nature or force of a belief that can confidently be pronounced identical to knowledge.

The authors' discussion of belief, which is really little more than an assertion of the sufficiency and philosophical invulnerability of belief, implicitly raises more issues than can easily be dealt with or than the authors remotely seem to recognize.[4] But paradoxically the emphasis on belief in the closing stages of "Against Theory" is not such as to compel an extended argument. Before it explicitly comes up, the question of belief has already been begged and defused to such a degree that it is scarcely a *question* any longer; moreover, the problems of belief and

---

4. The difficulty of response is compounded by the sudden and extreme dependence of the argument on work done by Stanley Fish in *Is There a Text in This Class?: The Authority of Interpretive Communities* ([Cambridge, Mass., 1980], pp. 350–71). It may seem almost necessary here to confront Fish directly; alternatively, Knapp and Michaels might claim that they are entitled to trade in the normal way on points established by Fish. Since a direct confrontation with Fish would require at least another essay, and since I do not acknowledge the appropriateness of the use to which his arguments are put in "Against Theory," I simply claim the right to limit liability to the authors.

Toward Uncritical Practice   63

knowledge are mischaracterized to such a degree that the triumph of belief is as facile as it is meaningless.[5] There is in effect nothing to engage with here other than the authors' assertion of the unsurpassable force of belief. I will however revert briefly to the wave-poem, approaching it now from the "belief" side rather than the "substance" side in the hope that that will enable me, if not to settle anything profound, then at least to suggest the insufficiency of pragmatic reliance on belief.

Epistemologically speaking, the pragmatist deduces from the example of the wave-poem that while we *believe* the poem to have been written by the wave we cannot interpret it, and it is correlatively disqualified as a poem. What makes all the difference, everywhere, all the time, to everything, is our possession by belief. No knowledge can transcend or replace belief, which accordingly constitutes the highest epistemological plane on which the human mind can function (as God in his own way said to Adam). What we happen to believe at a given moment about the authorship of the poem is absolutely determining. Knapp and Michaels acknowledge that the spectacle of a wave writing a poem might give rise to speculation—we might wonder, for example, if Wordsworth has become the genius of the shore, writing or perhaps reinscribing his poems from another plane of being—but such speculation must terminate in the *belief* that the wave has written the poem. Certainly no knowledge can come to our rescue; conversely, a "true" belief constitutes sufficient knowledge. And seeing, without too much ado, is believing.

But let us reconsider the sequence of events. We begin under the unquestioned (seemingly unquestionable) assumption that Wordsworth is the human author, presumed to have had effective intentions, of the poem. This unproblematical assumption, on which a whole interpretive practice may depend, is drastically challenged—shattered, denied— leaving us with a new belief about the poem that forecloses any further practice (all of which may reveal more about the limits of pragmatic interpretation than about those of interpretation in general, or reality in general). The submarine then appears, after which the status quo ante (or perhaps something equivalent to it) is restored, and enabling belief revives. What is the moral of the story?

A nonpragmatist might suggest that we have begun with an unquestioned belief or naive faith from which certain practices "naturally" follow. This belief is replaced not by just another belief but by an in-

---

5. This will no doubt seem prejudicial to the argument. But consider, for example, how we are told that a commitment to knowledge, as opposed to belief, leaves us only two ways to "go," either a "realist" way or an "idealist" way. The choice—the entire range of possibilities, discourses, interests—is thus typically narrowed down until it lies between a realism that, as defined, is wholly unphilosophical and an idealism that, as defined, is philosophically unrecognizable. Given such alternatives, belief is attractive. We may also choose to repudiate the zero-sum game in which belief (for reasons that I simply invite readers to examine) "wins" and knowledge "loses."

hibitingly negative belief *in relation* to the one first held. The effect this second belief produces is thus equivalent to a loss of faith in Wordsworth as author, in the poem as poem, and in our capacity to interpret. The appearance of the submarine may restore our faith and everything that depends on it. In other words, we have not passed through a simple succession of positive beliefs but have reverted to a belief (if that is still the word for it) that can never again be naive, unsuspecting, or natural. (In fact, it requires the spectacular artifice of the submarine *deus ex machina* to "save" our practice.) Maintaining our recovered power or determination to interpret following the traumatic shock of "ungroundedness"—following a revelation of the painful contingency of our practice—may require something more, or something other, than a childlike faith wedded to appearances.[6] It may even require that we reassess in general our position as authoritative interpreters, recognizing in it a presumption that needs to be either justified or abandoned.

No doubt this "requirement" will seem quixotically unreal—or incapable of being satisfied—in the institutional setting of literary interpretation; a degree of politic accommodation will thus have to be acknowledged. But the rejection of theory and corresponding exaltation of practice not only relaxes a constitutive tension within critical activity but also deprives practice of its primary source of justification. The practice envisaged will thus expose itself to charges of endless arbitrariness or redundancy, or it will be forced to invoke its own institutional existence as the "sign" of its legitimacy. In neither case will this "liberated" (ungoverned?) practice be capable of claiming status as a discipline, and it will in fact define itself as an indulgence or abuse to be tolerated.

6. The conception of belief as an innocent given and/or as a state of possession seems fundamental to antitheoreticalism. Like the "practi:e" it complements, "belief" is withdrawn from the structural oppositions as well as from the historical circumstances that might at once limit it and render it more meaningful. The authors also remain locked into a tautology in which what is truly believed becomes equivalent to truth, while truth becomes equivalent to whatever is truly believed. Finally, their conception of belief is one that assigns a kind of fullness and immediacy to the condition, whereas, almost by definition in our culture, "belief" has a proleptic character; a *lack,* even if only temporary, of justifying knowledge or "groundedness" is implicit in the conception. The verbal intensification of "belief" into "true belief" not only fails to solve the problem but opens up certain ironic vistas.

Truth or Consequences:
On Being Against Theory

Steven Mailloux

Before reading "Against Theory" by Steven Knapp and Walter Benn Michaels, I thought I fully understood Stanley Fish's theory of interpretive communities. Fish's theory seemed a consistent elaboration of the claim that there are no uninterpreted givens. What we take to be independent facts are actually constructions of our interpretive assumptions and strategies. From this perspective, texts do not determine interpretations; interpretations constitute texts. Furthermore, interpretive practices are never idiosyncratic; that is, acts of making sense are always a function of shared beliefs or interpretive conventions. Every individual interpreter is a member of an interpretive community: "Since the thoughts an individual can think and the mental operations he can perform have their source in some or other interpretive community, he is as much a product of that community (acting as an extension of it) as the meanings it enables him to produce."[1] Such a grounding of interpretation in communities defends this hermeneutic theory against the charge of relativism, the bugbear of the Anglo-American critical tradition since the heyday of New Criticism. New Critics claimed to avoid interpretive relativism by grounding meaning objectively in the autonomous text. Later, E. D. Hirsch tried to show that New Critical theory and practice resulted in the very relativism the New Critics abhorred; Hirsch argued that priority must be given to authorial intention in order to determine valid or correct interpretations. Fish's theory of interpretive communities holds that interpretation produces both textual meaning and

1. Stanley Fish, *Is There a Text in This Class?: The Authority of Interpretive Communities* (Cambridge, Mass., 1980), p. 14.

Reprinted from the June 1983 issue of *Critical Inquiry*.

authorial intention, but he avoids relativism by showing that there are
always correct interpretations, determined by communities rather than
individuals. Individual interpreters are not free to see or describe any
textual meaning they want—the fear of the New Critics—nor is meaning
made radically indeterminate—the complaint of Hirsch against the
anti-intentionalists. Rather, correct interpretations always exist and can
be (are already) determined. It's just that because interpretive communities can change, so too can what counts as a correct interpretation.

So went my understanding of Fish's position before reading
"Against Theory." However, I now see that this previous understanding
was incomplete. To approach "Against Theory" and eventually reveal *its*
incompleteness, we can begin with a literary example of the two hermeneutic accounts that Knapp and Michaels reject on their way to rejecting theory in general.

In George Orwell's *1984* the Party maintains its absolute power over
the people of Oceania by completely controlling all individual acts of
interpretation. Through material and ideological coercion, the Party
imposes its way of making sense on its people and achieves "the persis-
tence of a certain world-view and a certain way of life" which forms the
basis of its totalitarian rule.[2] This hermeneutic imperialism guarantees
that the people will continue to be "without any impulse to rebel" because
they are "without the power of grasping that the world could be other
than it is" (p. 173). O'Brien, the spokesman for the Party, points out the
philosophical assumption underlying its successful politics of interpretation: "Reality is inside the skull. . . . Nothing exists except through
human consciousness" (p. 218). Since the Party controls interpretation, it
controls human consciousness and thus manipulates reality itself. One
would-be rebel, Winston Smith, tries to resist the Party by attacking its
hermeneutics. He champions common sense, autonomous facts, external reality, and the empirical method. Though elsewhere Orwell supports Smith's philosophical stance, in *1984* he allows O'Brien to win the
argument (both rhetorically and politically) during the final confrontation between Smith and the Party spokesman.[3] O'Brien argues that "re-

2. George Orwell, *1984* (1949; New York, 1961), p. 173; all further references to this
work will be included in the text.
3. See Gerald Graff, "Politics, Language, Deconstruction, Lies, and the Reflexive
Fallacy: A Rejoinder to W. J. T. Mitchell," *Salmagundi* 47–48 (Winter-Spring 1980): 88–89.

Steven Mailloux, associate professor of English at the University of
Miami, is the author of *Interpretive Conventions: The Reader in the Study of
American Fiction.* He is currently at work on a book on the institutional
history of American literary criticism.

ality exists in the human mind, and nowhere else. Not in the individual mind, . . . only in the mind of the Party, which is collective and immortal. Whatever the Party holds to be truth *is* truth. It is impossible to see reality except by looking through the eyes of the Party" (p. 205). Smith is not able to counter O'Brien's arguments, and ultimately the Party is successful in achieving its goal: "We shall squeeze you empty, and then we shall fill you with ourselves" (p. 211). Smith submits by internalizing the Party's world view and adopting its hermeneutic theory.

It is inevitable that Smith must lose, not only because he confronts the overwhelming power of the state but also because he presents such a weak case for his hermeneutic position. As O'Brien points out, Smith holds that "the nature of reality is self-evident" (p. 205). He fails to understand that his commonsense "facts" are as much a product of interpretation as are the Party's; and he clings to a naive realist ontology and a simplistic commonsense epistemology that O'Brien demolishes from his dominant political position, through a more sophisticated hermeneutic argument, a form of idealism he calls "collective solipsism" (p. 219).

Knapp and Michaels would find neither Smith's realism nor O'Brien's idealism to be satisfactory as hermeneutic theories. They write that "a realist thinks that theory allows us to stand outside our beliefs in a neutral encounter with the objects of interpretation; an idealist thinks that theory allows us to stand outside our beliefs in a neutral encounter with our beliefs themselves" ("Against Theory," p. 27). A realist like Smith is mistaken when he assumes that "the object exists independent of beliefs" and that "knowledge requires that we shed our beliefs in a disinterested quest for the object" (p. 28). An idealist like O'Brien avoids this mistake when he implies that "we can never shed our beliefs," but he commits his own kind of error when he equates knowledge with "recognizing the role beliefs play in *constituting* their objects" (p. 28). This constitutive hermeneutics is a necessary corollary of both O'Brien's collective solipsism and Fish's theory of interpretive communities.[4] In the same way that O'Brien claims that the Party's collective mind creates reality, Fish argues that interpretive communities create what they claim merely to be discovering or describing. Of course, O'Brien and Fish perceive themselves as living within radically different arrangements of hermeneutic power. O'Brien sees himself as the extension of an interpretive community (the Party) that completely dominates the world of *1984*. Fish, on the other hand, claims that his world contains many competing communities, each vying for interpretive hegemony for its set of beliefs, values, and ideologies.

4. For discussions of constitutive hermeneutics, see my *Interpretive Conventions: The Reader in the Study of American Fiction* (Ithaca, N.Y., 1982), pp. 192–207, and "Learning to Read: Interpretation and Reader-Response Criticism," *Studies in the Literary Imagination* 12 (Spring 1979): 93–108.

Despite such differences in their sociological accounts, O'Brien and Fish end up in the same theoretical contradiction. During his debate with Smith, O'Brien's epistemological idealism leads him to imply that a true believer within the Party could somehow get outside the Party's belief system into a neutral space from which to judge the Party's beliefs. Knapp and Michaels argue that Fish makes a similar move when he claims to have a *theory* of interpretation through which he distances himself from his own interpretive assumptions. This theory allows him to argue that previous literary critics' "assumptions were not inferior but merely different" from his own.[5] As Knapp and Michaels point out, Fish is claiming here that "no beliefs are, in the long run, truer than others." But "it is only from the standpoint of a theory about belief which is not itself a belief that this truth can be seen" (p. 29). Since Fish himself admits there is no such standpoint outside belief, he has clearly contradicted himself. Theories like Fish's and O'Brien's which admit the absolute primacy of belief in practice cannot turn around and claim to escape belief in theory.

Knapp and Michaels ultimately argue that *all* theories cannot avoid similar contradictions or incoherencies whenever theory attempts to prescribe critical practice. They demonstrate how typical theorists base their methodological prescriptions on the prior separation of entities that are in fact logically inseparable (intention and meaning, language and speech acts, knowledge and true belief). Theorists make these false separations so that they can prescribe moving from one entity to the other to arrive at meaning or truth. Thus, if theory is understood as an attempt to describe so that it can have prescriptive consequences, then it is incoherent and should be abandoned. Theory, properly understood, has no consequences.

Knapp and Michaels' arguments are convincing as far as they go. Their attack on theory *as theory* (i.e., as it conceives itself) certainly showed me a contradiction in Fish's theory that I had previously failed to notice. However, the conclusion that Knapp and Michaels draw from their arguments—that theory is inconsequential and should therefore stop—does not necessarily follow. True, theory does not have consequences in the exact way it claims to have consequences. Nevertheless, theory has results of a very precise kind, as I will now try to show.

The work of Edward Said demonstrates quite clearly that theory can have disruptive consequences both inside and outside the discipline of literary studies. In *Orientalism* and other writings Said assumes a constitutive hermeneutics as he examines Orientalism as "the enormously systematic discipline by which European culture was able to manage—and even *produce*—the Orient politically, sociologically, militarily, ideologically, scientifically, and imaginatively during the post-

5. Fish, *Is There a Text?*, p. 368.

Enlightenment period."[6] Through Orientalism Europe imposed a self-serving meaning in an apparently disinterested way. In effect, it created an Orient that was ripe for domination. The imperialist West did exactly what the Party in *1984* tries to do: determine reality by controlling interpretation. The Party is simply more self-conscious about its "hermeneutics of power."[7]

Said's project has been to reveal the ideological interests behind the hermeneutic power of Western discourse about the Islamic Orient. But Said further claims that *all* descriptions of the Orient (not just those by European and American Orientalists) are perspectival constructions rather than objective representations:

> I do not mean to suggest that a "real" Islam exists somewhere out there that the media, acting out of base motives, have perverted. Not at all. For Muslims as for non-Muslims, Islam is an objective and also a subjective fact, because people create that fact in their faith, in their societies, histories, and traditions, or, in the case of non-Muslim outsiders, because they must in a sense fix, personify, stamp the identity of that which they feel confronts them collectively or individually. This is to say that the media's Islam, the Western scholar's Islam, the Western reporter's Islam, and the Muslim's Islam are all acts of will and interpretation that take place in history, and can only be dealt with in history as acts of will and interpretation.[8]

Since Said also grounds these acts of hermeneutic will in "communities of interpretation," his theory resembles the epistemological idealism of O'Brien and Fish, who claim that shared beliefs (assumptions, values, ideologies) constitute reality.[9] Though these theories are at times vulnerable to the "beliefless neutrality" objection discussed above, much more often they support assertions like Knapp and Michaels' that there is no "condition of knowledge prior to and independent of belief " (p. 26). If Knapp and Michaels are correct that "no general account of belief [similar to their own] can have practical consequences," then these idealist epistemologies that posit the primacy of belief should also be inconsequential (p. 28). But such accounts can and do have consequences. In the world of *1984,* the theory of collective solipsism provides a philosophical base for totalitarian domination. In the realm of American scholarship and politics, Said's theoretical assumptions guide his practical analyses of Orientalism, and these analyses have had very definite consequences as the debates within the *New Republic,* the *New*

6. Edward W. Said, *Orientalism* (New York, 1978), p. 3; emphasis added.
7. The term is Graff's in "Textual Leftism," *Partisan Review* 49 (1982):566.
8. Said, *Covering Islam: How the Media and the Experts Determine How We See the Rest of the World* (New York, 1981), p. 41. See also *Orientalism*, pp. 273 and 322.
9. Said, *Covering Islam,* p. 41.

York Review of Books, History and Theory, and other journals testify. Indeed, a recent Humanities Report article noted that "the position Said represents [in Orientalism] has produced a set of semi-academic study groups and has implications for government and foreign policy."[10]

But how exactly can a hermeneutic theory that, according to Knapp and Michaels, should have no consequences result in these rhetorical and political effects? In Said's case, the reason is that when he reveals Orientalist representations as based on interested belief rather than impersonal truth, objectivists read his demystifying project as (successfully or unsuccessfully) undermining the validity of Orientalist interpretations, and Orientalism's victims read this same project as providing support for the objectivity of their own self-interpretations. These appropriations of Said's discourse can occur because a demonstration that others' asserted truth is actually interested belief always counts as a critique of their assertions in the present arena of critical and political discussion. In such an arena, to expose asserted truth as "mere" belief is to have the effect of undermining that truth even though the debunker elsewhere insists that all truth is perspectival belief. Even in an essay in which Said foregrounds the perspective from which he makes his analysis (e.g., in "Zionism from the Standpoint of Its Victims"), his discourse still has the rhetorical effect of proof or propaganda (depending on whether the reader is convinced or not by his arguments).[11]

But political consequences are only the most far-reaching results of theory. More limited but just as real are the effects of theoretical prescriptions within the discipline of literary studies. Even if it is granted that all theories are based on logical mistakes (like separating intention and meaning), theories still have consequences for critical practice. All we need do is remember the effects of New Critical proscriptions against the intentional and affective fallacies. The critics persuaded by these theoretical prohibitions avoided extrinsic approaches and directed their analyses to intrinsic elements in the literary text itself—image patterns, symbolic structures, and so forth. More recently, theories of undecidability have changed the interpretive practices of many within the discipline: instead of looking for unities, they look for disunities, contradictions, incoherencies. Theory does change practice.

Here we finally reach the limits of Knapp and Michaels' account of theory. Their description turns out to be as incomplete as my previous understanding of Fish's work was incomplete. Theory does claim to be what Knapp and Michaels define it as, but theory actually functions differently. In fact, theory is a kind of practice, a peculiar kind because it claims to escape practice. But the impossibility of achieving this goal does

10. Colin R. MacKinnon, "Talking Back: Orientalism and the Orientals," Humanities Report 4 (Feb. 1982): 5.
11. See Said, "Zionism from the Standpoint of Its Victims," Social Text 1 (Winter 1979): 7–58; rev. and rpt. in Said, The Question of Palestine (New York, 1979), pp. 56–114.

not prevent theory from continuing, nor does it negate the effects it has *as persuasion*. It is telling that Knapp and Michaels do not call for the end of critical practice even though they reject criticism's claim to find meaning objectively in autonomous texts, intentions, or reading experiences. Michaels has pointed out correctly that such practice misconceives its function: the meanings it claims to find are actually determined completely by the beliefs it assumes.[12] Similarly, theory claims to be in a neutral position beyond belief and turns out not to be, yet as theoretical practice it can still affect other practices as persuasion. Theory can simply continue doing what all discursive practices do: attempt to persuade its readers to adopt its point of view, its way of seeing texts and the world. Whether successful persuasion takes place as a result of misunderstanding or not, theory can be consequential as rhetorical inducement and thus will never be abandoned (as Knapp and Michaels no doubt realize).

In their conclusion to "Against Theory," the authors write:

> The theoretical impulse, as we have described it, always involves the attempt to separate things that should not be separated: on the ontological side, meaning from intention, language from speech acts; on the epistemological side, knowledge from true belief. Our point has been that the separated terms are in fact inseparable. It is tempting to end by saying that theory and practice too are inseparable. But this would be a mistake. Not because theory and practice (unlike the other terms) really are separate but because theory is nothing else but the attempt to escape practice. Meaning is just another name for expressed intention, knowledge just another name for true belief, but theory is not just another name for practice. [Pp. 29–30]

Though they deny it here, Knapp and Michaels do seem to separate theory and practice. They could have said that "theory is just another name for metapractice (practice about practice)." Instead they chose to imply a distinction between two kinds of discourse that are similar in function: theory is an instantiation of practice even as it claims to escape from practice. Why do Knapp and Michaels ignore this? Strangely, this implied separation of theory and practice can be seen as strengthening rather than weakening their argument. Indeed it confirms at least part of it. Like all theoretical discourse, "Against Theory" separates the inseparable—theory from practice—in order to prescribe practice—the abandonment of theory. Of course, whether Knapp and Michaels' theory has consequences depends on whether it persuades readers to take its amusing examples and ingenious arguments seriously. I hope I have done so.

12. See Walter Benn Michaels, "Saving the Text: Reference and Belief," *MLN* 93 (Dec. 1978): 771–93.

Lost Authority: Non-sense, Skewed Meanings, and Intentionless Meanings

Hershel Parker

In their attempts to clarify and improve upon some of the arguments of E. D. Hirsch and his recent follower P. D. Juhl, Steven Knapp and Walter Benn Michaels refer to "the meaning of a text" without asking how the text reached the state in which they encounter it. In this they follow Hirsch and Juhl. Defining the argument of *Validity in Interpretation* as "unabashedly and I think necessarily theoretical," Hirsch paid almost no attention to the possible implications of evidence about the history of a text (except in some offhand speculations which strike me as more incisive and ultimately more fruitful than anything American textual theorists were then saying).[1] It was without recourse to evidence of composition, revision, and transmission that Hirsch defined "textual meaning as the verbal intention of the author" and treated "a text" or "the text" as an immutable arrangement of words, if not punctuation marks also.[2] In asking what we are appealing to when we appeal to the text, Juhl likewise did not allow for a challenge of, Which text?—not even when he went so far as to insist that the meanings of minor textual details are intended by the author.[3] Echoing Hirsch, Knapp and Michaels insist

1. E. D. Hirsch, Jr., *Validity in Interpretation* (New Haven, Conn., 1967), p. x. The speculations I refer to are on p. 233: "With a revised text, composed over a long period of time (*Faust*, for example), how are we to construe the unrevised portions? Should we assume that they still mean what they meant originally or that they took on a new meaning when the rest of the text was altered or expanded?"
2. Ibid., p. 224.
3. See P. D. Juhl, *Interpretation: An Essay in the Philosophy of Literary Criticism* (Princeton, N.J., 1980), pp. 66–89 (the title of chap. 4 is "The Appeal to the Text: What Are We Appealing To?"); see also in chap. 6 the subsection "Are the Meanings of Textual Details Unintended?," pp. 129–32.

Reprinted from the June 1983 issue of *Critical Inquiry*.

that "the meaning of a text is simply identical to the author's intended meaning" and that "all meaning is always the author's meaning" (pp. 12, 14–15). Echoing Juhl, they insist that "all local meanings are always intentional" (p. 18 n.8). For Knapp and Michaels there can be, in short, no "intentionless meanings" (p. 15).

As a textual scholar I applaud Knapp and Michaels for admitting the existence of the author and welcoming him back from the banishment first imposed by the New Critics and then reimposed by subsequent critical juntas. But their arguments against theory do not, empirically speaking, get us much farther than the theories of Hirsch and Juhl, and for much the same reason—the failure to pay attention to what lessons can be learned from "particular texts" (p. 11). One lesson is that authorial meaning is not something an author pours into literary work when putting on the last touch, as Michael Hancher seems to argue.[4] Still less can intentionality be conferred upon a literary work at the moment of publication, as James Thorpe so magisterially contends.[5] Rather, as John Dewey says, meaning is infused into the text at the moment each part is written. The "artist is controlled in the process of his work by his grasp of the connection between what he has already done and what he is to do next." He must "at each point retain and sum up what has gone before as a whole and with reference to a whole to come"; if this does not happen, there will be "no consistency and no security in his successive acts."[6]

Writers repeatedly fail to achieve their intended meanings during the actual creative process, even though their control over the emerging work is then at its strongest. At best, as Murray Krieger argues, they turn these failures of original intention into opportunities for success in some unexpected direction, but flaws which result from shifting or imperfectly realized intentions commonly survive in the printed text in the form of "contrary details" which we override in our compulsion to make sense of what we read.[7] If writers fail to achieve their intentions during composi-

4. See Michael Hancher, "Three Kinds of Intention," *MLN* 87 (Dec. 1972): 827–51 (see p. 831 n.10, for Hancher's only mention of authorial intention during the process of composition).
5. See James Thorpe, *Principles of Textual Criticism* (San Marino, Calif., 1972), p. 38.
6. John Dewey, *Art as Experience* (New York, 1934), pp. 45, 56.
7. See Murray Krieger, *Theory of Criticism* (Baltimore, 1976), p. 27, for the unlooked-for opportunity; and p. 41, for the reader's compulsion to make sense of texts.

Hershel Parker is H. Fletcher Brown Professor in the department of English, University of Delaware. After a year as a fellow in Delaware's Center for Advanced Study, he is completing a manuscript on literary authority, an analysis of aesthetic implications of textual criticism on American fiction.

tion, they are even more likely to damage parts of what they had achieved when they belatedly alter a text, whether at someone else's suggestion or at some whim of their own. In revising or allowing someone else to revise a literary work, especially after it has been thought of as complete, authors very often lose authority, with the result that familiar literary texts at some points have no meaning, only partially authorial meaning, or quite adventitious meaning unintended by the author or anyone else. For my own convenience I will cite examples from standard American novels, but it would be equally easy to find examples in other genres and other national literatures.[8]

Often part of a text we read (and write about) has no meaning at all. In chapter 16 of *Huckleberry Finn,* Huck and Jim are going downriver at night on the raft, having unknowingly passed Cairo in the fog. In one paragraph they plan to watch for a light so Huck can paddle ashore in the canoe and ask someone how far down the river Cairo is, and in the next paragraph Huck concludes that there "warn't nothing to do, now, but to look out sharp for the town, and not pass it without seeing it." This nonsense was created when Twain agreed to drop from between the two paragraphs the raftsmen episode, which contained the reason for the decision not to ask anyone else but just to watch out for the town.[9] In *Pudd'nhead Wilson,* as we have long known, several passages refer to the Italian twins in ways that make sense only if they are conjoined, as they were (two heads, four arms, one trunk, two legs) when the original version was completed.[10] In chapter 13 of the published novel a meaningless passage occurs not involving the twins. A delegation of Democrats calls upon Wilson, the village butt, a lawyer who has just tried—and lost—his first case during his more than two decades in Dawson's Landing, and offers to support him for mayor. These men look like fools afflicted with a political death wish, but Wilson's desirability as a candidate survives from the original version, where he had just been catapulted into popularity by successfully defending his first client, the twin Luigi, against the charge of kicking Tom Driscoll (his case resting,

8. I deliberately choose examples from a text Walter Benn Michaels cites in "*Sister Carrie*'s Popular Economy" (*Critical Inquiry* 7 [Winter 1980]: 373–90) and examples from *Tender Is the Night,* celebrated by a coeditor of *Critical Inquiry,* Wayne C. Booth, in *The Rhetoric of Fiction* ([Chicago, 1961], pp. 190–95).

9. See Peter G. Beidler, "The Raft Episode in *Huckleberry Finn,*" *Modern Fiction Studies* 14 (Spring 1968): 11–20.

10. I briefly comment on *Pudd'nhead Wilson* in "'The 'New Scholarship': Textual Evidence and Its Implications for Criticism, Literary Theory, and Aesthetics," *Studies in American Fiction* 9 (Autumn 1981): 181–97; a long essay on *Pudd'nhead* is forthcoming in the (tardy) Autumn 1981 issue of *Resources for American Literary Study.* See also Philip Cohen, "Aesthetic Anomalies in *Pudd'nhead Wilson,*" *Studies in American Fiction* 10 (Spring 1982): 55–69. In this response to Knapp and Michaels I am not always distinguishing between anomalies which were created by the addition of the Roxy-Tom plot as the manuscript was being completed in December 1892 and the anomalies which were first introduced in July 1893 when Twain pulled out half of his typescript for publication as *Pudd'nhead Wilson.*

of course, on the impossibility of proving which twin did the kicking). Chapter 17 of Stephen Crane's *Maggie* was rendered meaningless in the Appleton edition (1896) by the excision of the title character's climactic encounter with the huge fat man. In this strange text, Maggie no longer explicitly goes down to the dark river, with anyone else or alone, but tall buildings magically jump down there from their place back within the final block.[11] The Appleton edition of *The Red Badge of Courage* (1895) also contains meaningless passages, such as this sentence in the last chapter, which has no possible referent for the plural "matters": "There were small shoutings in his brain about these matters."[12] In a recent example, the Dial version of Norman Mailer's *An American Dream,* the hero, Stephen Richards Rojack, speaks out of "that calm" when there is no previous mention of a calm in that scene.[13]

Often enough revised texts will contain passages which make a minimal kind of sense but lack the specific meaning they were invented to convey, even when that meaning is literally their reason for being. In *Pudd'nhead* the twins are present at all only because when conjoined they had for months served Twain as a source for hilarious inventiveness, and taking them out of the final text would have required more work than he was willing to perform. Once the twins are (most of the time) separated, Luigi's kick becomes commonplace, and other passages are lifeless: Twain would never have had the twins play duets on the piano if they had not had four hands to put on the keyboard and only one bottom to sit on. (The book illustration shows one twin sitting on the piano stool and one on a chair—no fun at all.)

Clues to specific authorial meanings are sometimes removed with enough of the context left for the reader to arrive at a vague sense of the authorial meaning, although not the precise meaning the author had intended, as in this sentence from *Sister Carrie:* "In her own apartments Carrie saw things which were lessons in the same school."[14] Since the 1900 edition omits the one and two-thirds pages which Dreiser wrote to precede this sentence, the reader has to undergo a process of imperfect

11. See Parker and Brian Higgins, "Maggie's 'Last Night': Authorial Design and Editorial Patching," *Studies in the Novel* 10 (Spring 1978): pp. 64–75.

12. I first suggested reconstructing the manuscript version of *The Red Badge of Courage* in *Nineteenth-Century Fiction* 30 (March 1976): 558–62. For a full discussion, see Henry Binder, "The *Red Badge of Courage* Nobody Knows," *Studies in the Novel* 10 (Spring 1978): 9–47, rpt. in his edition of *Red Badge* (New York, 1982).

13. See my "Norman Mailer's Revision of the *Esquire* Version of *An American Dream* and the Aesthetic Problem of 'Built-in Intentionality,' " *Bulletin of Research in the Humanities* 84 (Winter 1981).

14. Theodore Dreiser, *Sister Carrie,* ed. James L. W. West III and Neda M. Westlake, Pennsylvania Edition (Philadelphia, 1981), p. 102, and *Sister Carrie,* ed. Donald Pizer, Norton Critical Edition (New York, 1970), p. 77. The Pennsylvania Edition is based upon a fresh transcription of the manuscript, the Norton upon the much-abridged first edition (1900).

self-correction which the author did not set up: he has to assume that "lessons" refers to the conclusion of the once-distant paragraph which now stands just in front of the sentence in question, specifically to the law that "If a man is to succeed with many women, he must be all in all to each." Then, as he proceeds, he is forced to revise that conclusion and take "lessons" as referring rather vaguely to the longings awakened by the sight of prosperous people, but he could never arrive at the original lessons about the crucial difference between having money and being poor. Any resemblance to the process of reading as described by Stanley Fish is coincidental: this is a case of needless, unintended fumbling ignorantly imposed upon the reader by careless excision.[15]

Sometimes a passage in a text will embody two different and contradictory authorial intentions rather than one. For the English edition of *White-Jacket*, Melville added to chapter 27 two new short paragraphs, the second of which is this: "And the only purpose of this chapter is, to point out as the peculiar desert of individuals, that generalized reputation, which most men, perhaps, are apt to ascribe in the gross, to one and all the members of a popular military establishment."[16] Purpose not being a quality which can be infused into an unrevised passage by an act of retro-declaring or retro-wishing, no one assigned to define the purpose of the chapter as Melville first wrote it could possibly come up with any such definition. In the passage from *Maggie* discussed earlier, the revision was designed to keep the text from meaning what it had too obviously meant, and small attention was given to making it mean anything at all in its reduced form, much less to making it mean something else in particular; but in the Appleton *Red Badge of Courage*, where a similar disregard prevailed for what if anything was left of the meaning after the original, objectionable meaning was removed, there was also a deliberate effort to impose a new meaning on the remnants of the original meaning by the addition of a perfunctorily upbeat last paragraph: "Over the river a golden ray of sun came through the hosts of leaden rain clouds." Yet throughout the chapter and the earlier portions of the text as printed in 1895, clues to Henry Fleming's vanity and self-delusion survive despite the excision of the most blatant evidence. The result of the Appleton expurgation was a maimed text which reached classic status because of the power it still retained but which, once the vogue of close reading set in during the 1940s, became the ground on which a

15. Compare the meaning and effect of the "mental conflict" Carrie experiences in the Pennsylvania Edition (p. 91) with that she experiences in the Norton (p. 71). In the Norton, the reader can scour the preceding page and then correctly deduce that the voice of conscience is in conflict with the voice of want, but Dreiser wrote "mental conflict" to refer to the dialogue between the voices in the immediately preceding twelve paragraphs, not a word of which is retained in the 1900 text which the Norton follows, a text which does not carry full and precise authorial intentionality.

16. See my "Melville and the Concept of 'Author's Final Intentions,' " *Proof* 1 (1971): 165–66.

generation of critics battled inconclusively, armed with contradictory indications in the text.

Sometimes passages embodying one authorial meaning are so placed as to read as if they embodied a different one. What we know as chapter 11 of *Pudd'nhead* was written when Tom was merely a local white youth, a sneak thief and a scamp. In the published book, "Tom" from the start is not Tom at all but a changeling, part black and a slave, and chapters 9 and 10 deal with his learning the horrible truth and undergoing great, if temporary, anguish about the news. In writing what is now chapter 10 Twain took some pains to make it plausible that in later scenes Tom would act much as usual, despite his brief mental turmoil, but he did not bother to work Tom's new condition into the parts already written. When he put *Pudd'nhead* together, he hoped in a general way that Tom would seem black in the passages written when he was all white, but he did not make any attempts to *make* him black in those passages, not even perfunctory attempts such as he made to separate the twins in passages where he retained them as characters. As it turned out, Twain got an accidental bonus on the level of local meaning, for any reader of chapter 11 will think that Tom snatches away his hand so the palm-reading Wilson will not find out that he is part black and a slave, not merely that Wilson will find out that he is a thief. Judging from the abundant evidence that Twain did not read entirely through what he salvaged as *Pudd'nhead Wilson,* he probably did not ever specifically "intend" the new meaning of the gesture, even retroactively, although he would have been delighted to get something for nothing. Judging from the contemporary reception and from modern academic criticism, there was no need for the author to have invested any more labor on the salvage operation than he did, for no critic has complained about Tom's being distractingly white in some middle chapters of the book.

Adventitious meanings of scenes in altered texts are more often than not out of keeping, despite the happy fate which befell Tom's gesture. An example occurs in *Pudd'nhead* near the beginning of chapter 13, written when Tom was still white and the rival with the fairer of the conjoined twins, Angelo, for the affections of Rowena, the daughter of the twins' landlady, who is, of course, as white as Tom. Moping along a lane, Tom thinks of calling on Rowena in order to have some "cheerful company," then realizes that "the detested Twins would be there." Seeing Tom's unhappiness, Wilson starts to ask if Rowena has rejected him, but Tom explains that the trouble is that he has been disinherited by Judge Driscoll, his real uncle when the passage was written. Twain was not titillating himself and his readers with violating the taboo against allowing a black to harbor casual thoughts of a flirtation with a white girl; rather, in slapping together a salable text, Twain simply failed to notice that the earlier written passage had accrued unintended racial implications.

Inadvertent, intentionless meanings riddle the 1951 edition of *Tender Is the Night,* the one which Malcolm Cowley reordered chronologically in accordance with an intention Fitzgerald had had at some point in his last years, well after the publication of the book in 1934.[17] This text is in fact a showcase of adventitious meanings which the author could not possibly have intended and could not have wanted if he had become aware of them. They range from large-scale inadvertencies (such as the ludicrousness of the long mystery about what happened in the bathroom at the Villa Diana, when every reader of the reordered text knows just what kind of mad scene Nicole had enacted there) to small-scale inadvertencies (such as the luridness which accrues to the screening of Rosemary's movie, *Daddy's Girl,* once every reader knows that Nicole, who is watching the movie, was driven insane by committing incest with her father). Dozens of local details lose precise authorial meanings and seem to gain nonauthorial meanings, even though almost all the words of the original text are retained. Authorial functions for parallel scenes, for instance, are subtly altered when the scenes are spaced either further apart or closer together, and authorial functions are altered even more drastically when scenes, images, and words are reordered, so that the reader encounters what was meant as an echo before encountering the occurrence which the echo was designed to recall.

More recently, in revising the *Esquire* version of *An American Dream,* Mailer made some tiny excisions which reduced the mutual awareness of male characters and thereby altered the characters' functions in unintended ways. The ex-prizefighter Romeo, for instance, inadvertently rises in the hierarchy of characters; it is no longer clear that the contest Rojack has with Romeo is meant as a kind of hysterical parody of the more significant contest that has just occurred between Rojack and Detective Roberts, a psychological equal of the hero in the serial but not explicitly so in the book.

As these examples suggest, nonmeanings, partially authorial meanings, and inadvertent, intentionless meanings coexist in standard literary texts with genuine authorial meanings. It happens all the time, and almost nobody minds. Now and again a critic will even take the trouble to celebrate adventitious meaning over what the author really intended, all in the name of respecting the authority of the author ("It's his text, isn't it?"). One pious critical argument is that if an author "accepts an editorial change or suggestion, his acceptance is the equivalent of a creative act, even though the act is the initial responsibility of an editor."[18] Editorial theorists have made scripture of a rationale of copy-text which cannot accommodate cases of revision because it as-

17. See Higgins and Parker, "Sober Second Thoughts: Fitzgerald's 'Final Version' of *Tender Is the Night," Proof* 4 (1975): 129–52.
18. Pizer, "On the Editing of Modern American Texts," *Bulletin of the New York Public Library* 75 (Mar. 1971): 148.

sumes, contrary to all we know about the creative process, that an author's creative state of mind, and therefore his authority over the text, is sustained indefinitely, throughout a lifetime.[19] We all have a long way to go before we can talk confidently about the authority of the author. One could start that hazardous journey by taking quite literally the truism that literary criticism depends upon textual scholarship. So does literary theory—which will no doubt continue to flourish despite the ingenuous pleas of Knapp and Michaels.

19. See W. W. Greg, "The Rationale of Copy-Text," *Studies in Bibliography* 3 (1950–51): 19–36. The best description of the creative process I have seen, aside from some comments by literary men and women, is Albert Rothenberg, *The Emerging Goddess: The Creative Process in Art, Science, and Other Fields* (Chicago, 1979), esp. chap. 13, "Goddess Emergent: Creative Process and Created Product," pp. 345–80.

What I say here about the author's final intentions differs somewhat from what Steven Mailloux extrapolates from my earlier comments in his *Interpretive Conventions: The Reader in the Study of American Fiction* (Ithaca, N.Y., 1982), p. 112 n.51. What's wrong with modern editorial theory is that it is incompatible with what we know about the finality of decisions made during the creative process.

On the Theory of "Against Theory"

Adena Rosmarin

Steven Knapp and Walter Benn Michaels begin their argument "Against Theory" by announcing that "the object of our critique is not a particular way of doing theory but the idea of doing theory at all" (p. 11). The object of my critique is to show that what Knapp and Michaels are arguing against is indeed "a particular way of doing theory" and that their attack on *theory* fails precisely insofar as this is so.

They divide their argument into two parts. In the first they discuss what they call "the ontological side of theory—its peculiar claims about the nature of its object" (p. 24). In the second they discuss "theory's epistemological project": the attempt "to base interpretation on a direct encounter with its object, an encounter undistorted by the influence of the interpreter's particular beliefs" (p. 25). The purpose of this division is to enable an analogy: "If the ontological project of theory has been to imagine a condition of language before intention, its epistemological project has been to imagine a condition of knowledge before interpretation" (p. 25). The "mistake" of ontology is to imagine an intentionless language, the "mistake" of epistemology to imagine a beliefless knowledge. Knapp and Michaels argue that there are no such things: that language without intention is not language, it only "resembles" language; that knowledge separate from belief is not only not knowledge, it is not possible. Thus they conclude:

> The theoretical impulse, as we have described it, always involves the attempt to separate things that should not be separated. . . . Our point has been that the separated terms are in fact insepa-

Reprinted from the June 1983 issue of *Critical Inquiry*.

rable . . . and that the theoretical enterprise should therefore come
to an end. [Pp. 29–30]

As their definition of "epistemology" and "ontology" reveal, Knapp
and Michaels take their notion of theory from philosophy as it was in-
stitutionalized by Kant's followers in the nineteenth century: a project
whose business is the grounding and adjudicating of claims to knowledge, where "knowledge" is defined as the accurate representation of
what is known. In this they are right. Our discipline *has* envisioned itself
as the progressive acquisition of knowledge about literary texts, and
literary theory *has* assumed the grounding and adjudicating role of philosophy. It asks: Where is the essence (ground) of literary meaning lo-
cated? How do we most accurately represent it? Which interpretations
are the most accurate representations? A set of answers to these questions is what we call a "poetics," and there are many such sets: affective,
intentional, semiological, ideological, formalist, psychoanalytic, and so
on.

Knapp and Michaels are wrong, however, to see this way of doing
theory as more than a way. It is simply our way, and so it has come to
seem the thing itself. Richard Rorty makes precisely this point vis-à-vis
philosophy's image of itself as a theory of representation.[1] His massive
and persuasive critique may be therapeutically transferred to the
essentially philosophical enterprise of literary theory, demystifying its
present and seemingly given embodiment, suggesting new and less vulnerable ways of talking about interpretation. The representational tradition begins with Plato's choice of an ocular metaphor for the process of
knowing, with the notion that knowledge is the result of a face-to-face
encounter with the object known. (Note that we still routinely say "I see"
for "I understand.") The tradition grows increasingly epistemological as
it moves through Descartes and Locke to Kant, the Platonic search for
accurate representations of what is outside the mind modulating into a
search for privileged inner representations and then into a search for
the mental rules constituting those representations. Although Kant directed this search toward propositional rather than perceptual knowledge, his advance remained within the framework of such causal
metaphors as "constitution," "making," and "synthesizing." Traditional
philosophy continued—and continues—to define itself as a search for

---

1. See Richard Rorty, *Philosophy and the Mirror of Nature* (Princeton, N.J., 1979).

Adena Rosmarin is assistant professor of English at the University
of Miami. The present essay is an excerpt from her forthcoming book
Rhetorical Poetics. She is currently working on a study of the relation of
interpretive history and critical explanation.

the ground or cause of knowledge and for the traceless way of representing or knowing that ground.

This, then, is the model of literary theory that Knapp and Michaels argue against: it aims to find the object which compels belief (hence the "peculiar claims"), to "base interpretation on a direct encounter" with that object, to expunge the "interpreter's particular beliefs." One wonders, however, why Knapp and Michaels assume the separation of theory's ontological and epistemological projects since in the Kantian model that they attack the two are joined. One also wonders why in the ontological part of their argument they collapse the radical and currently ubiquitous distinction between positive and negative hermeneutics, between those who believe in the possibility of grounding interpretation and those who don't. For the latter move, at least, they give a reason.

According to Knapp and Michaels, "positive" theorists such as E. D. Hirsch and P. D. Juhl *add* intention (in the form of "authorial intention" or "speech acts") to language in order to ground meaning whereas "negative" theorists such as Paul de Man *subtract* intention in order to preserve "the purity of language from the distortion of speech acts" (p. 21). But despite their difference, both acts separate the supposedly inseparable; both make the "mistake" of the "theoretical impulse." Showing the similarity of these different acts is essential to showing that theory, not just a particular way of doing theory, is mistaken, but the similarity will only seem significant if we are made strongly aware of the difference. Realizing this, Knapp and Michaels devote the first two-thirds of their essay to displaying that "the positive theorist adds intention, the negative theorist subtracts it" (p. 24). They then direct us to a footnote:.

> At least this is true of the present generation of theorists. For earlier theorists such as W. K. Wimsatt and Monroe C. Beardsley, the objective meanings sought by positive theory were to be acquired precisely by *subtracting* intention and relying on the formal rules and public norms of language. [P. 24 n.16]

While one must applaud the intellectual fastidiousness which led to the inclusion of this qualification, even in a footnote, one must wonder how the authors failed to see what its inclusion does to their argument. If negative hermeneutics is definitively distinguished from positive hermeneutics by its habit of subtracting intention from language, how can the same procedure define the positive theory of Wimsatt and Beardsley? Since the space of a generation can hardly alter what Knapp and Michaels present as philosophically definitive matters, one must fault the definition. But since it is this definition which enables them to argue that theory makes the same "mistake" across the hermeneutic board, that it is not just a way of doing theory but theory itself which is mistaken, faulting the definition must render their entire argument suspect.

Let us focus this suspicion on their premises, the two points which Knapp and Michaels take as self-evident. First, they announce that "the issues of belief and intention are . . . central to the theoretical enterprise; our discussion of them is thus directed not only against specific theoretical arguments but against theory in general." Second, they announce that intention and language, like belief and knowledge, "are in fact inseparable." Since theory functions by mistakenly "splitting apart" these terms, and since these terms are "central to the theoretical enterprise," these two assumptions should give Knapp and Michaels their argument—but only if we accept them (p. 12).

Granted, intention and belief have been and are central to certain theoretical arguments—especially and not incidentally to those Knapp and Michaels use as examples—but they are by no means central to all. Many have thought that literary meaning is grounded in or, what is the same, explained by what it imitates. Such mimetic objects include not only authorial intention but also ideas, actions, "general nature," the feelings or imagination of the poet, and mental and natural processes. Others have thought that literary meaning is explained by its internal structures, or by the activity of reading, or by convention systems. Unless Plato, Plotinus, Aristotle, Johnson, Wordsworth, Shelley, Coleridge, Holland, Iser, and Culler—to select but a few from among the advocates of such groundings—are to be seen as not doing theory, then arguing against "theory in general" by arguing against only intention and belief must be less than persuasive.

Equally unpersuasive is their claim that language and intention are "in fact inseparable." As their examples are meant to show, contemporary theory commonly separates them. Even if Knapp and Michaels are right to argue that such separation is wrong, the burden of proof still rests with them, and they rather too obviously attempt to unburden themselves by begging the question, by assuming what needs proving. If we leave the contemporary scene and recall, however briefly, the history of this issue, the burden even more strongly demands bearing. Would Plato in the *Phaedrus* be so concerned about writing were language and intention inseparable? Is it not the potential independence of the written word, its tendency to take off and lead a life of its own, that is the cause of so much ancient worry and so much recent delight? Recall also the Renaissance obsession with binding words (*verba*) to what they represent (*res*): "Ye man also take heid," warns King James, "to frame your wordis and sentencis according to the mater." "Those words . . . are best," cautions Fulke Greville, "which doe most properly expresse the thought." It "is the first distemper of learning when men study words and not matter," announces Francis Bacon, "for words are but the images of matter."² Why all the fuss if words and things or, to take the Knapp and Michaels version of this venerable dualism, language and intention are either inseparable or thought to be so? Their choice of premises displays—or assumes—an ignorance of the historical and contemporary contexts in which they write.

There must be a better way of talking about theoretical activity than that offered by Knapp and Michaels: that Hirsch "has failed to understand the force of his own formulation," that Fish "fails to recognize the force of his own discussion of belief" (pp. 13, 26–27). Rather than assuming that two of the most intelligent, sophisticated, and self-conscious practitioners of literary theory don't know what they are doing, let us assume that they—along with Wimsatt and Beardsley, Juhl, and de Man—do. And let us further assume—as Knapp and Michaels urge—that what these theorists are doing is essential to the theoretical project as traditionally defined. These assumptions make possible another way of talking about theoretical activity.

It would go something like this: Hirsch, Wimsatt and Beardsley, Juhl, de Man, and Fish are all seeking an interpretive ground, the cause of literary meaning. They find it in various places, places which are definitively needless of definition but definitively needy of protection against contamination from another ground or from a representing medium. For de Man, as for all formalists, however radical, this ground is the language of the text. He accordingly resists any other grounds—such as speech acts—which would constrain the independence and diminish the stature of his. He also resists the contaminating presence of the reader, arguing that "the reading is not 'our' reading, since it uses only the linguistic elements provided by the text itself."³ Wimsatt and Beardsley find their ground in "the formal rules and public norms of language." Fish finds his ground first in the textual features which control the reader's experience and later in the "interpretive strategies" which control that experience and thereby constitute the text.⁴

Although interpretive grounds are always presented as self-

2. King James VI, "Ane Schort Treatise," in *Elizabethan Critical Essays*, ed. G. Gregory Smith, 2 vols. (London, 1904), 1: 217; Fulke Greville, "A Treatie of Humane Learning," *Poems and Dramas of Fulke Greville, First Lord Brooke*, ed. Geoffrey Bullough, 2 vols. (New York, 1945), 1: 181; Francis Bacon, *The Advancement of Learning*, ed. William A. Wright (Oxford, 1970), p. 20. For a tracing of the *res/verba* pairing through the quattrocento see Bernard Weinberg, *A History of Literary Criticism in the Italian Renaissance*, 2 vols. (Chicago, 1961). For the later history of the pairing see A. C. Howell, "*Res et Verba*: Words and Things," *ELH* 13 (Mar. 1946): 131–42.

3. Paul de Man, "Semiology and Rhetoric," in *Textual Strategies: Perspectives in Post-Structuralist Criticism*, ed. Josué V. Harari (Ithaca, N.Y., 1979), p. 138.

4. See Stanley Fish, *Is There a Text in This Class?: The Authority of Interpretive Communities* (Cambridge, Mass., 1980) and, in particular, his introductory explication of these two groundings.

evident—indeed, they are powerful insofar as they seem to be so—in practice they must be argued for, defended against other contenders for the honor. The characteristic initial move of the theorist is accordingly an attempt to displace the institutionally "in place" ground. Thus Hirsch leads off his argument for "Objective Interpretation" by attacking René Wellek and Austin Warren's *Theory of Literature,* Wimsatt and Beardsley's "The Intentional Fallacy," and William Empson's *Seven Types of Ambiguity.*[5] Thus Fish builds his case for "Literature in the Reader" by attacking Wimsatt and Beardsley's "The Affective Fallacy."[6] Hirsch and Fish mount these particular attacks because, when they wrote, interpretive authority was lodged in the language of the text, and these were the theoretical texts which put it there.

The attack in both cases proceeds by dissociation and fusion. Hirsch does, as Knapp and Michaels argue, treat language and intention as if they were separate, but he does so only initially and with good reasons: first, his audience thought they were separate, and, like all good rhetoricians, Hirsch begins by standing with his audience; second, their supposed separateness enables his powerfully persuasive move of unification. As he himself tells us, his argument is "an attack on the view that a text is a 'piece of language' and a defense of the notion that a text represents the determinate verbal meaning of an author."[7] Fish initially discusses reader, text, and authorial intention as if they were separate, but like Hirsch he does so, first, because that is how his audience saw them and, second, because their seeming to be so enables the unification move: "This, then, is my thesis: that the form of the reader's experience, formal units, and the structure of intention are one, that they come into view simultaneously, and that therefore the questions of priority and independence do not arise."[8] My analyses are meant to suggest that what Knapp and Michaels treat as inherent and erroneous dissociations might be more subtly and profitably discussed as analytic strategies, effective ways of dismantling previous grounds and clearing space for new. They are also meant to suggest that theory, even representational theory, is hardly the unsubtle and unaware enterprise that Knapp and Michaels think it is.

Knapp and Michaels conclude by criticizing Fish's separation of knowledge and belief, a separation they find to be the epistemological analogue of the ontological separations perpetrated by Hirsch et al. They approve Fish's collapse of knowledge and belief but disapprove as Fish steps back to describe this collapse, a description that proceeds, as do all descriptions, under the aegis of "knowing" rather than "believing."

5. See E. D. Hirsch, Jr., "Objective Interpretation," *Validity in Interpretation* (New Haven, Conn., 1967), p. 226.
6. See Fish, "Literature in the Reader: Affective Stylistics," *Is There a Text?*, pp. 21–67.
7. Hirsch, *Validity in Interpretation,* p. 226.
8. Fish, "Interpreting the *Variorum,*" *Is There a Text?*, p. 165.

They think that this procedure introduces conceptual wrinkles into Fish's literary theory but fail to note that Fish is no longer doing *literary* theory. He has moved up to a metacritical level (Knapp and Michaels record in a footnote that Fish tells us this) from which he looks down upon an explicitly *critical* ground, the "interpretive strategies" which determine our critical agreements and disagreements. His project now becomes the representation of this new ground, and to be persuasive he must seem to describe it without contamination from the representing medium or, what is here the same, *his* "strategies." Obviously, ground and medium have been collapsed, as they always are in theories whose represented objects are interpretive procedures—as in Kant, as in Fish. Although this collapse does not create the problems of representational theory, it does foreground them, drawing attention to the medium which always leaves contaminating traces, to the ground which is infinitely regressive, which can only be "stopped" by a methodological contradiction.[9] But Fish's project is self-consciously rhetorical rather than philosophical; it only masks as philosophical to appropriate persuasive clout. As a way of talking about literature, representational theory is powerful *because* it is seemingly philosophical, and it becomes mistaken only when we forget that this seeming is just that and no more. Fish is not thus forgetful, but his theoretical finesse escapes Knapp and Michaels. Because it does, it also escapes them that his project is as fully "ontological" or descriptive of a ground as those which they describe. Their separation of ontology and epistemology proves no more rigorous than their unification of positive and negative hermeneutics.

The Knapp and Michaels argument against theory fails, then, on several counts. It argues against a *way* of doing theory and not against "theory in general." While representational theory can be faulted logically, aesthetically, and ethically, Knapp and Michaels not only fail to show such faults, they fail to show that this way of talking is the only way that we have had or can have. Their attack proceeds by unifications and dissociations which their own (significantly footnoted) commentary reveals as faulty. Their premises beg their question. Finally, they engage in the very moves they find so mistaken in others. Thus they argue that language and intention are inseparable because words, once separated from intention, are no longer really words: "They will merely seem to *resemble* words" (p. 16). Now how do Knapp and Michaels know *this?* Well, of course, they don't. But in order to mount their argument they must make this move, just as Hirsch et al. must make similar dissociations in order to begin talking. The growing suspicion that Knapp and Michaels are engaging in the very enterprise that they are attacking is right: "Against Theory" is a thoroughgoing theoretical argument. It has

9. See Michael McCanles, "The Authentic Discourse of the Renaissance," *Diacritics* 10 (Spring 1980): 77–87, for an excellent unfolding of the "infinitely regressive ground" problem as it troubles historical criticism.

an object: the theoretical "impulse" or "mechanism" which "causes" our "mistakes." Their examples "represent" their ground and, as such, are meant to compel our belief: "Our examples are meant to represent the central mechanism of all theoretical arguments, and our treatment of them is meant to indicate that all such arguments will fail and fail in the same way" (p. 12). (Including theirs?) Their object suffers the reduction suffered by all objects in the process of representation, the only *complete* representation being a copy. Their medium is as transparent, as deferential to its object as possible—hence their strategically lucid, frequently ingenuous, at times condescending prose.

The question of alternative theories remains, and while a few paragraphs can hardly begin to entertain answers, I will suggest the direction one such answer might take. We could begin with Rorty's suggestion that we substitute *conversation* (with each other, including past "others") for *confrontation* (with the object) as "the ultimate context within which knowledge is to be understood."[10] Adapted to literary theory, Rorty's suggestion might unfold like this: rather than reducing literary texts and their readers to the stable and schematized constructs so necessary to representational theory, a theorist might postulate texts of both inexhaustible richness and affective power, and readers of unlimited imaginative sophistication. He would try to put together a theory which would make discussion of such texts and readers possible. He would be after a *way of talking* rather than (although it might include) a *way of looking*. Since richness and power are what attract us to literature, and imaginative sophistication is what results from that attraction, the only reason not to begin with these is representational theory's abhorrence of change, ineffability, complexity, uniqueness, and, in sum, all that makes reading and talking about literature interesting and important, all that makes them so difficult to *represent*.

One important result of freeing ourselves from the representational bind, from the compulsion to judge accuracy or correctness, has been noted by Fish. When reading the works of previous theorists and critics, we would be able to " 'regard those performances not as unsuccessful attempts to approximate our own but as extensions of a literary culture whose assumptions were *not inferior but merely different*' " (p. 27). Knapp and Michaels quote this passage (I repeat their emphasis) and then comment:

> To imagine that we can see the beliefs we hold as no better than but "merely different" from opposing beliefs held by others is to imagine a position from which we can see our beliefs without really believing them. To be in this position would be to see the truth about beliefs without actually having any—to know without believing. [P. 27]

10. Rorty, *Philosophy and the Mirror of Nature*, p. 389.

To know without believing and, presumably, to believe without knowing are for Knapp and Michaels self-evidently impossible states. But where is it written that this is so? I'm sure that everyone can think of at least one place where precisely the opposite is written, for example, in Shakespeare's sonnet 138: "When my love swears that she is made of truth, / I do believe her, though I know she lies." The relationships between believing and knowing, loving and misrepresenting (conflated in "lies"), cursing and promising (conflated in "swears") are vertiginous, but they are not beyond our capacity to enact or discuss, only beyond the capacity of representational theory.

The literary text is neither as simple as this theory requires, nor are we as simpleminded. Because it is only this *way* of talking that cannot cope with linguistic, emotional, and intellectual dexterity, with our capacity to read, talk, and live "as if," it is tempting to conclude as Knapp and Michaels conclude: by arguing that representational theory "should therefore come to an end" (p. 30).[11] But there is no need to call a halt to a powerful, if imperfect, enterprise. All we need do is recognize this way of doing theory as just that—a way. All we need do, in other words, is put it in its hermeneutic place.

11. The "as if" alludes to Hans Vaihinger, *The Philosophy of "As If": A System of the Theoretical, Practical, and Religious Fictions of Mankind,* trans. C. K. Ogden, 2d ed. (London, 1949).

Intentionless Meaning

William C. Dowling

It has occurred to me a number of times in the years I've been reading *Critical Inquiry* that the "Critical Response" section ought perhaps to be accompanied by another simply entitled "Scholia": a place for unpolemical remarks on arguments set forth in earlier issues. In any event, I want to be clear at the outset that what follows isn't prompted by anything like disagreement or discontent with Steven Knapp and Walter Benn Michaels' exciting article, the implications of which readers are surely still assimilating. My remarks are intended (fateful word!) precisely as scholia, concerning one technical, one historical matter.

The technical matter is this: Knapp and Michaels get a certain amount of rhetorical mileage out of the repeated claim that authorial intention ("the author's intended meaning," as they phrase it) and textual meaning are identical, and by so doing they turn against E. D. Hirsch what has always been his only real weapon in the wars over intentionality; but the rhetorical gain comes, I think, at the cost of a point that won't stand up to closer logical scrutiny. There is, it seems to me, a kind of too-hasty conceptual elision going on in the claim that "once it is seen that the meaning of a text is simply identical to the author's intended meaning, the project of *grounding* meaning in intention becomes incoherent" (p. 12).

It is the first part of this assertion that gives pause: to say that either of two terms—here, intention and meaning—is entailed by the other is not, surely, to say that one is identical with the other, and in all sorts of cases the distinction turns out to be logically significant. By simply collapsing one term into the other in the way they do, Knapp and Michaels

Reprinted from the June 1983 issue of *Critical Inquiry*.

in effect deprive one or the other term of any independent function. Yet in this sort of situation, one ought to bear in mind Wittgenstein's injunction that if everything behaves as though a sign has meaning, then it does have meaning. "Intention" and "meaning" behave, at any rate, as though they had independent meanings.

The business of mutual entailment, on the other hand, is tricky enough to *look* like an identity of the two terms involved in many cases, which is why the point often gets fudged in arguments of the sort that Knapp and Michaels are making. I'm reminded of a story told by a friend of mine about a philosophy seminar he once took with John Searle. The discussion was about the concept of promising, and my friend was having difficulty with how, at a certain point in the act of promising, a new thing called an "obligation" materializes out of nowhere. Where does it come from? Searle's instant rejoinder was: "Look, Schueler: you're in a football game. Your quarterback hands you the ball. You zig; you zag; you run into the end zone. Where do the six points come from?"

A witty rejoinder, as one expects from Searle, but on examination it seems only to translate the original difficulty into other terms: Where, indeed, *do* the six points come from? Yet this football analogy does demonstrate why it is so easy to mistake, in such cases, mutual entailment for identity: we might want to say, put to the question, that what we meant by "touchdown" was just running into the end zone under conditions specified by the rules of the game. Here we have something almost perfectly analogous to what Knapp and Michaels want to say about the identity of intention and meaning. Still, such mutually entailed terms as "promise" and "obligation," "intention" and "meaning" do, under closer scrutiny, retain a stubborn logical independence from each other.

"Promising," in fact, may be taken to illustrate the point. If for purposes of discussion we allow "obligation" to mean only that form of obligation that ensues from having made a promise (as opposed to other, more general kinds of obligation, such as being dutiful to one's parents, etc.), it seems reasonably clear that promise and obligation are never simply different names for the same thing: my obligation to help you paint your kitchen on Saturday is not identical with the act I performed in promising you to do so, if only because the obligation persists when the act is over. (The distinction in this case is between a state and an act:

William C. Dowling, associate professor of English at the University of New Mexico, is the author of *The Critic's Hornbook* and the forthcoming *The Boswellian Hero.* He is currently working on "the epistolary moment," a critical study of the verse epistle in England between 1660 and 1800.

obligation as a *state* that ensues from the *act* of promising or having promised.)

This is the sort of mutual entailment that Knapp and Michaels are trying to put their finger on; what they want to say is not that meaning and intention are identical but that there is something incoherent in any attempt to treat one independently of the other. My obligation to help you paint your kitchen may not be identical with my promise to do so, but it is quite meaningless to speak of my having that obligation if I have made no promise to do so. Conversely, it makes no sense for me to speak of having made you a promise if I do not recognize the act as having bound me to an obligation. What we are dealing with, in short, is the complicated logic of a situation in which either of a pair of terms is rendered meaningless when treated in isolation from the other.

Knapp and Michaels almost say this, in fact. One passage early in their essay might be regarded as their retreat from the "identity thesis," the first sentence being a mistaken formulation of the relation between intention and meaning, the second being a formulation that, because it does not assert identity, gets that relation exactly right:

> The mistake made by theorists has been to imagine the possibility or desirability of moving from one term (the author's intended meaning) to a second term (the text's meaning), when actually the two terms are the same. One can neither succeed nor fail in deriving one term from the other, since to have one is already to have them both. [P. 12]

Because identity and mutual entailment behave so much alike, moreover, Knapp and Michaels' larger argument survives their blurring of the distinction.

All this is worth going into, I think, because it accounts for a historical asymmetry in Knapp and Michaels' theory of the intention-meaning controversy: Hirsch's intentionalist theory of meaning is opposed to those of various contemporary critics, like Paul de Man and J. Hillis Miller, whose notion of indeterminate meaning testifies to the recent influence on Anglo-American criticism of various continental schools of theory. Yet Hirsch's original argument was of course not directed at these critics and in fact appeared when such movements as post-structuralism were not yet a cloud on the Anglo-American horizon (interestingly enough, Hirsch's *Validity in Interpretation* and Derrida's *De la grammatologie* appeared in the same year, 1967). One must look elsewhere for the original targets of Hirsch's argument.

Hirsch's real opponents in 1967 were, of course, W. K. Wimsatt and Monroe C. Beardsley, whose famous article on the intentional fallacy in effect founded formalism as a school of criticism and whose account of objective meaning remains a classic of modern theory—so much a classic, in fact, that one might have expected it to have received a more extended treatment from Knapp and Michaels. Yet Wimsatt and Beardsley get only a belated footnote, and a quite misleading account of their position: "For . . . W. K. Wimsatt and Monroe C. Beardsley, the objective meanings sought by positive theory were to be acquired precisely by *subtracting* intention and relying on the formal rules and public norms of language" (p. 24 n.16).

It might be, of course, that Wimsatt and Beardsley are mentioned so perfunctorily because their argument, made nearly thirty years ago, can be regarded as something of a museum piece. I don't think so, though. I think that Knapp and Michaels, quite properly excited at having worked through to an important new insight into the intention-meaning problem, and also having failed to distinguish between identity and mutual entailment, failed to see that they had discovered just the point that gave Wimsatt and Beardsley's argument in "The Intentional Fallacy" its power. In effect they show why that argument worked.

As I've suggested, the reason that Knapp and Michaels were led in the first place to speak repeatedly of "the author's meaning" is undoubtedly that Hirsch does so throughout *Validity in Interpretation,* and it is an incoherence in Hirsch's argument they want to expose. Moreover their asserting an identity between intention and meaning allows them to do this without embarrassment. But as soon as they actually turn to discussing an instance of ambiguous or disputed meaning, their terms shift in a certain significant way. "Author" becomes "speaker":

> For a sentence like "My car ran out of gas" even to be recognizable as a sentence, we must already have posited a speaker and hence an intention. Pinning down an interpretation of the sentence will not involve adding a speaker but deciding among a range of possible speakers. Knowing that the speaker inhabits a planet with an atmosphere of inert gases and on which the primary means of transportation is railroad will give one interpretation; knowing that the speaker is an earthling who owns a Ford will give another. But even if we have none of this information, as soon as we attempt to interpret at all we are already committed to a characterization of the speaker as a speaker of language. [P. 14]

It was precisely the distinction between author and speaker that licensed close reading as a distinctively formalist or New Critical mode of interpretation: one was to stop asking what Marvell meant or intended to mean in "To His Coy Mistress" and ask what the speaker (a voice or presence "internal to the poem") was saying or trying to say. Knapp and Michaels are quite right in saying that Wimsatt and Beardsley wanted to get rid of authorial intention; that was, so to speak, the negative part of the formalist program. It was balanced, though, by the positive demand that the literary work be reconceived in dramatic terms as having an internal speaker, audience, and so on.

The great virtue of Knapp and Michaels' account of intention is that it allows us to see just how this notion of an internal speaker is more than just a convenient New Critical metaphor: since meaning must always *in purely formal terms* involve intention (as opposed to intention as the prior psychological state of a deceased author) and since where there is an intention there must always be an intender, interpretation must begin by positing something like the internal voice or speaker of formalist theory. What their account makes plain, once the notion of mutual entailment is substituted for that of identity, is that "speaker" is not just one of the necessary fictions of discourse abstractly conceived but an invariant condition of any possible mode of discourse.

In a sense, then, Knapp and Michaels' extremely perceptive discussion of indeterminate meaning can be viewed almost as a rudimentary exercise in formalist interpretation. Consider, in light of that discussion, such a sentence as "I was whipped." The fact that it can mean "I was lashed with thongs" or "I was badly beaten in a tennis match" or "I was extremely tired" (and not some entirely different meaning like "I wanted a vanilla ice-cream cone") shows that (1) certain rules of determinacy are already in force and (2) that an account of meaning *already* assumes that an intention (somebody intending to mean something) is also present. As Knapp and Michaels make clear, what is added when we learn that the speaker is a sadomasochist, a tennis player recounting a weekend match, or a tired commuter returning from the city is not an intention but information about an intention.

The discovery that information about an intention was invariably information about an internal speaker lay at the heart of the formalist program of objective interpretation. The theoretical interest of such sentences as "I was whipped" is that they are short enough to look fairly indeterminate; any expansion ("I was whipped when I got onto the 5:36 for Greenwich and ordered a martini; fifteen minutes later I felt better") moves us toward the clearly defined "internal" speaker of formalist theory. (Stanley Fish is great at figuring out ways to suggest that this principle is false, but even he would have trouble if we were allowed to expand indefinitely and at will the sort of example utterances he favors.)

A revised history of formalism, then, might look something like this: at the level of practical interpretation, close readers like Cleanth Brooks had discovered that positing the existence of the sort of internal intention Knapp and Michaels talk about sets in motion a complex dialectic of objective inference; the more one could discover about this intention the more one knew about a speaker internal to the work, and the more one knew about this speaker the more one knew at any given moment about his intention, and so on. Thus the speaker of "To His Coy Mistress" emerged as a young man of a certain level of education and breeding trying to persuade a beautiful young woman of his own social class of the wisdom of their sleeping together.

This was the context, in turn, in which authorial intention began increasingly to look dispensable in any account of objective interpretation: Knowing all this about the speaker of "To His Coy Mistress"—and being aware, moreover, that all this would remain true if it should come to light that someone other than Marvell actually wrote the poem—could one really learn anything more, or anything essential, by inquiring into "Marvell's intention"? More than an inaugurating manifesto, "The Intentional Fallacy" was a coup de grâce to the crude intentionalism associated with an older genetic or biographical criticism. What Knapp and Michaels make clear is that the formalist argument succeeded in its season by exploiting to the fullest an intentionality that is already and inevitably entailed by the very notion of meaning.

A Reply to Our Critics

Steven Knapp and Walter Benn Michaels

What are the consequences of "Against Theory"?[1] According to E. D. Hirsch, the "most probable effect is to foster the comforting idea that there's no point in pursuing historical scholarship" (Hirsch, p. 51). According to Jonathan Crewe, "Against Theory," taken "seriously enough," "would entail a significant, and in my view retrogressive, change in professional attitude"; it would establish "an ideology under which a privileged status quo would be secured against fundamental questioning" (Crewe, pp. 53, 54). According to William C. Dowling, "Against Theory" shows the essential correctness of the New Critical distinction between author and speaker and therefore has the consequence of promoting a "formalist program of objective interpretation" (Dowling, p. 93). According to Daniel T. O'Hara, the "rhetorical effect" of "Against Theory" "is essentially nihilistic"; "by clearing the air of theory," we have "taken away from students the means necessary to do criticism at all" (O'Hara, pp. 37–38).

This list of consequences is interesting for several reasons. First, its diversity: the proposed consequences range from technical problems of critical method, to questions of professional politics, to fundamental issues in epistemology. More interesting than their diversity, however, are their problematic relations. Where Dowling thinks "Against Theory"

1. We wish to thank our respondents for their discussions of the issues raised in "Against Theory." Many of our friends and colleagues have commented less formally on our arguments; we would like to thank especially Paul Alpers, Donald Davidson, Frances Ferguson, Joel Fineman, Stanley Fish, Michael Fried, Catherine Gallagher, Gerald Graff, Stephen Greenblatt, Richard Grusin, Geoffrey Hartman, Jeffrey Knapp, Ruth Leys, Ralph Rader, and Jane Tompkins.

Reprinted from the June 1983 issue of *Critical Inquiry*.

supports arguments for a mode of objective interpretation, Hirsch thinks it discourages what he takes to be the only possible mode of objective interpretation, historical scholarship. Where Crewe thinks we defend the critical status quo (what he later calls "business as usual" [p. 58]), O'Hara thinks we make any critical practice impossible. But from our standpoint, neither the diversity nor the problematic character of these consequences is particularly significant. For the possibility of deriving *any* of these consequences from "Against Theory" would already amount to a radical objection to an argument that explicitly denies having any consequences for the practice of literary criticism. Since, in our view, theory precisely consists in the attempt to derive practical consequences from general accounts of interpretation, having such consequences would mean that "Against Theory" had inadvertently turned theoretical. If any one of the consequences alleged by our critics does indeed follow from "Against Theory," then our claims are mistaken, our arguments against theory should be abandoned, and our attack on theory should come to an end.

The consequences alleged to follow from "Against Theory" fall into three general categories: epistemological, methodological, and professional. We will address each of these in turn.

1. Epistemology

The only epistemological claim in "Against Theory" is that true belief and knowledge are the same. What follows from this claim, we argued, is that the traditional project of justifying beliefs by appealing to sources of knowledge independent of belief (e.g., sense data) is incoherent. We argued further that recognizing the incoherence of this project in no way affects our ordinary sense of the difference between true and false beliefs. Imagining that an identification of knowledge and true belief in any way prevents one from having true beliefs only makes sense if one remains committed to the project of justifying beliefs by appealing to independent sources of knowledge.

Most of our critics who are concerned with epistemology seem to

Steven Knapp is an assistant professor of English at the University of California, Berkeley; his book *Personification and the Sublime: Milton to Coleridge* is forthcoming. **Walter Benn Michaels,** an associate professor of English at the University of California, Berkeley, is working on the relation between literary and economic forms of representation in nineteenth-century America.

agree that independent sources of knowledge are unattainable. But they disagree with our claim that nothing else follows from this fact. Crewe, for example, never argues for the possibility of grounding beliefs in some independent source of knowledge. Nevertheless, discovering the "ungroundedness" of belief constitutes, for him, a "traumatic shock" that "may even require that we reassess in general our position as authoritative interpreters, recognizing in it a presumption that needs to be either justified or abandoned" (Crewe, p. 64). Crewe, that is, thinks that "ungrounding" our beliefs jeopardizes our interpretive authority—our sense that we know what a text means. Since knowing what a text means consists in having true beliefs about it, Crewe presumably thinks that either we must be able to justify our beliefs (and hence our interpretations) by grounding them in something more fundamental than belief—or we must abandon them. And since Crewe makes no argument for the possibility of justifying our beliefs in this way, it would seem to follow that we should give them up.

In our view, while one can give up particular beliefs (i.e., change one's mind), one cannot give up beliefs in general. Crewe agrees that belief is inescapable. But whereas we are untroubled by the ordinary fact that people can change their minds, Crewe thinks that the possibility of replacing one belief with another reveals "the painful contingency of our practice" (Crewe, p. 64). Why "painful"? Because, he thinks, the fact of any one of our beliefs turning out to be false suggests the fundamental unreliability of *all* our beliefs. But why should a particular case of being wrong call all our beliefs into question? Why, for example, should discovering that what looked like a poem really wasn't require us to "reassess in general our position as authoritative interpreters"? For Crewe, discovering that an apparently true belief has turned out to be false means discovering that an apparently *grounded* belief has turned out to be *ungrounded*. A belief is true, according to Crewe, only if it is grounded, that is, secured against all possibility of correction. But since no belief really can be grounded (all beliefs are corrigible, any particular belief might turn out to be false), then, following Crewe's logic, no belief can really be true.

Crewe, then, ends up equating groundedness and truth. But for this equation to make any sense, we must after all be able to stand outside our beliefs in order to distinguish between the ones that only seem true and the ones that really are true—the ones that only seem grounded and the ones that really are grounded. Crewe, however, never offers any argument to show that a position outside belief is possible; in fact, as we have noted, he doesn't seem to think it is. This coincidence of a desire to escape belief and a conviction that we can't do so no doubt accounts for the unusual tone of his response to "Against Theory." Perhaps the most extreme symptom of Crewe's dilemma is his invention of the "negative belief": to change one's mind, according to Crewe, is to replace a belief "not by just another belief but by an inhibitingly negative belief *in relation* to the one first held" (pp. 63–64). Changing one's mind cannot, he thinks, be described as passing "through a simple succession of positive beliefs." But what Crewe calls a "negative belief *in relation* to the one first held" is simply a positive belief (in the way that all beliefs are positive) that the first belief was false. A belief that something is *not* the case is not a negative belief that something *is* the case. Only an intense desire to escape beliefs could make one imagine that calling them "negative" makes them any the less beliefs.[2]

Because "Against Theory" denies the possibility of escaping beliefs, Crewe thinks it has the epistemological consequence of condemning us to "precritical primitivism." Thus, he remarks at one point, what might have been "a timely move beyond theory turns out in fact to be a return to a condition 'before' theory" (p. 55). Earlier in the same paragraph, however, Crewe asserts that "the antitheoretical argument" could only "rank as a contribution . . . *in* the field of critical theory, from which it never escapes." And, in fact, several of our critics derive the epistemological consequences of "Against Theory" from a claim that our arguments remain theoretical. According to O'Hara, our "position against theory depends entirely on assumptions that are theoretical" (p. 33 n.4); according to Adena Rosmarin, " 'Against Theory' is a thoroughgoing theoretical argument" (Rosmarin, p. 86); according to Steven Mailloux, "Against Theory," "like all theoretical discourse," attempts to "prescribe practice" (Mailloux, p. 71).

The claim that an argument against theory is itself theoretical seems odd, and neither Crewe nor O'Hara advances any argument to support it. Perhaps they think that to say anything at all about theory is to be a theorist. But this is like saying that to argue against astrology is to be an astrologer. Rosmarin and Mailloux, on the other hand, do provide arguments to support their characterization of "Against Theory" as theoretical.

For Mailloux, the very persuasiveness of "Against Theory" makes it theoretical. Mailloux is convinced by our argument that "all theories are based on logical mistakes" (Mailloux, p. 70). He denies, however, that such mistakes prevent theory from having practical consequences. Indeed, for Mailloux, theory is paradigmatic of "all discursive practices"—inevitably including "Against Theory" (Mailloux, p. 71). Theory, like all discourse, claims for its arguments the force of objective

2. In criticizing our account of belief, Jonathan Crewe complains that our sketches of realism and idealism are "unphilosophical" and "unrecognizable" respectively (Crewe, p. 63 n.5). They certainly are incomplete, but the distinction between regarding "the real object" as the external "cause" (*res extra animam*) of knowledge and as the "normal product of mental action"—of the "consensus or common confession that constitutes reality"—is a familiar one in philosophy. The account just cited is from the writings of Charles Sanders Peirce (*Collected Papers of Charles Sanders Peirce*, ed. A. W. Burks, Charles Hartshorne, and Paul Weiss, 8 vols. [Cambridge, Mass., 1931–58], 8:15–17) but is by no means unique to Peirce.

demonstration; its logical mistakes belie this claim but in no way diminish its true power "*as persuasion*" (Mailloux, p. 71).[3]

There are several ways to interpret Mailloux's claim that mistakes can have consequences. If he means, for example, that people can have false beliefs and can act accordingly, we agree. People can believe in astrology and order their lives in accordance with astrological predictions. But the case of theory is different in at least one important respect from that of astrology. Believers in astrology can in fact follow the recommendations of their charts, but believers in theory cannot, in our view, follow the methodological prescriptions that theory claims to generate. Theoretical mistakes thus have no consequences for the practice of literary criticism, but they do of course bear on the practice of theory itself. Believers in a particular theory may write articles about it, give lectures on it, teach courses in it. And not only can theoretical mistakes have consequences; so can pointing them out. Thus "Against Theory" indeed has consequences—but only for the practice of theory. If this is what Mailloux means, we still agree.

But this cannot be what Mailloux means, since the conclusion he draws from "Against Theory" is the opposite of ours. According to us, "Against Theory" shows that theory should be abandoned; according to Mailloux, "Against Theory" shows that theory "will never be abandoned" (Mailloux, p. 71). What we think we have shown is that one way of talking about literary criticism is mistaken; what Mailloux thinks we have shown is that theory, in being mistaken, is like every way of talking about everything. Mailloux's position, in other words, is not merely that an argument against astrology is a form of astrology but that *every* argument is a form of astrology—that is, all arguments are equal and equally mistaken. For Mailloux, the consequence of this discovery, as we noted earlier, is that all arguments can only function as persuasion, never as demonstration. But once one knows that all arguments are equally mistaken, how can they function even as persuasion? In what sense can one be persuaded of something that one knows all along is false? How can one be persuaded and not persuaded at the same time? To imagine yourself in this condition is to imagine yourself being persuaded while looking at persuasion from the outside. And to imagine yourself looking at persuasion from the outside is to put yourself in the position we attributed to Stanley Fish—looking at your beliefs without really believing them. Having acknowledged the contradiction in Fish's theory,

3. Adena Rosmarin relies on essentially the same distinction but substitutes "representation" for demonstration and "conversation" (a term she borrows from Richard Rorty) for persuasion (see Rosmarin, pp. 81, 87). For Rosmarin, as for Steven Mailloux, all argument must be based on the illegitimate but necessary claim to "know" something: illegitimate because no one really *can* know anything, necessary because without the claim to know something, we cannot "begin talking." Since we indeed claim to know something, Rosmarin finds in "Against Theory" an example of the mechanism that makes all theoretical argument possible and thus takes us to be "engaging in the very enterprise that [we] are attacking" (Rosmarin, p. 86).

Mailloux thus repeats it, choosing demonstration over persuasion as Fish chose knowledge over belief.

It may seem paradoxical that Mailloux's announced preference for persuasion ends up committing him to demonstration—to argument independent of rhetorical inducement. But this choice is an inevitable consequence of separating what should not be separated. Once one thinks that persuasion has no relation to truth, its persuasiveness vanishes, leaving nothing but demonstration, even if the only thing that can be demonstrated is the emptiness of persuasion.

Mailloux, unlike Crewe, thinks himself content to settle for persuasion or belief. But in the end, like Crewe, he finds himself committed to the traditional ideal of objective knowledge, even if Mailloux's knowledge is as empty of content as Crewe's negative beliefs. Crewe, Mailloux, and Rosmarin are all negative theorists of the sort we described in "Against Theory" (see pp. 24–25). What their example shows is that negative theory requires a commitment to objectivity (knowledge without beliefs) as great as that of positive theory. With enemies like these, objectivity doesn't need friends.

As negative theorists, these critics have a particular view of the relation between theory and practice. Their hostility to the traditional project of grounding beliefs in knowledge makes them skeptical of the claims of interpretive method—that is, the claims of theory to guide practice.[4] But their continuing sense that beliefs are inadequate forces them to imagine an empty version of the position occupied by the traditional methodologist. From the negative theorist's position, theory cannot guide practice but merely testifies to its inevitable failure. For the negative theorist, the truth discovered by theory is that all interpretations are equally false, and the consequences of this discovery are purely affective: Mailloux is happy, Crewe is sad. But our position, which identifies true belief with knowledge, leaves untouched the ordinary notions of true and false and thus gives no occasion either for pleasure or regret.

2. Method

Not all of our critics are willing to surrender the traditional claims of method. Hirsch, Dowling, and Hershel Parker all agree with each other

4. Rosmarin claims to detect a confusion in our distinction between positive and negative theory (see pp. 82–83). She is puzzled by our footnote identifying W. K. Wimsatt and Monroe C. Beardsley as positive theorists despite the fact that they recommend "*subtracting* intention and relying on the formal rules and public norms of language" ("Against Theory," p. 24 n.16). But Rosmarin has misunderstood our distinction. What makes someone a positive theorist is not a particular attitude toward intention but a belief that *any* recommendation about intention—whether to add or to subtract it—could provide a method for achieving correct interpretations. The source of Rosmarin's confusion seems to be the accidental fact that current anti-intentionalists, such as Paul de Man, tend also to be negative theorists.

and with us that there can be no meaning without intention, but they disagree with the argument of "Against Theory" at what Hirsch rightly calls "its most novel and crucial point": its insistence on "the practical nullity of the idea of intention" (Hirsch, p. 49). Far from accepting our claim that the idea of intention is useless as a guide to practice, each of these critics derives from this idea a methodological project. For Hirsch, the centrality of intention shows the importance of historical scholarship; for Parker, the "lesson" of intentionalism is that "literary criticism depends upon textual scholarship" (Parker, p. 79); for Dowling, our arguments about intention show that "interpretation must begin by positing something like the internal voice or speaker of formalist theory" (Dowling, p. 93). Clearly these projects fall into two categories, historical and formalist.

The historical project rests on a claim about evidence—namely, that certain kinds of documents (letters, diaries, manuscripts, etc.) are particularly relevant to determining the meaning of literary texts. It might seem plausible to suppose that an identification of meaning with the author's intention provides theoretical support for the historian's sense of the value of such documents. While historical evidence of this kind might well be valuable, nothing in the claim that authorial intention is the necessary object of interpretation tells us that it is. In fact, nothing in the claim that authorial intention is the necessary object of interpretation tells us anything at all about what should count as evidence for determining the content of any particular intention. To think, for example, that only the poem and no other document should count as evidence of the poet's intention is just as consistent with the thesis that intention is necessary. Recognizing the inescapability of intention doesn't tell us which documents, if any, are the important ones. One could believe that all poetry in every language and every age was written by a universal muse and that therefore no information about any other person could be of any possible interpretive interest—and this too would not be incompatible with the necessity of intention.

Given that there is no relation between recognizing the necessity of intention and knowing what should count as the best interpretive evidence, why does a historically minded critic like Hirsch continue to think that the idea of intention has any practical relevance? The answer is that Hirsch thinks that recognizing what he calls the "formal necessity" of intention "at every moment of interpretation" still leaves the interpreter free to choose between what the "composer of the text intended" and what " 'some postulated author is intending it to mean' " (Hirsch, pp. 49, 50). This seems to us a puzzling distinction. What can the word "author" mean if not the composer of the text? In our view, to "postulate" an author is already to commit oneself to an account of the composer of the text, and there is nothing to choose between them because they are the same. But Hirsch, whose central claim in his response to

"Against Theory" is that "critical practice" and "meaning" are "what we choose to make" them, needs the distinction because he needs the choice (Hirsch, p. 52). Hirsch needs, in other words, a counterexample to our claim that understanding the meaning of a text can only be understanding what its author intended.

Hirsch takes his example from the career of William Blake:

> When Blake re-authored his 1789 *Songs of Innocence* in 1794, he didn't change the texts of the poems at all. But his second interpretation was not the same as "what the author intended" in his first interpretation. In 1794 Blake believes that what he now intends is not what he then intended in 1789 by his text. [Hirsch, p. 51]

The fact that Blake's intention in 1794 is not the same as it was in 1789 shows, according to Hirsch, that it is possible to interpret a text while disregarding "what we believe its author meant in composing it."

But what does this example really show? If Blake in 1794 is viewed simply as the reader of the 1789 *Songs,* then he has merely misinterpreted his own earlier work. This doesn't show that we can interpret a text without interpreting it as what we believe its author meant. It only shows that we can misinterpret what the author meant. The example is complicated, however, by the fact that Blake in 1794 is not simply rereading the *Songs of Innocence* but rewriting them (though without changing the "texts" of the 1789 version). But if he is in fact rewriting them, then the poems of 1794 are different poems from those of 1789, and the meaning of the 1789 *Songs* is irrelevant. Why does Hirsch think it remains relevant? He must continue to think that the two works are the same. If they *are* the same, Hirsch believes he has found a genuine instance of an interpreter (Blake) knowing the author's intention and interpreting the text without regard to that intention. But why would one call this interpretation? What makes this any different from the case of the critic who, knowing what the text really means, nevertheless prefers his mistake?[5]

The difference in this case is that the critic happens to be the author of the original text—a fact that matters only if he is not simply rereading his text but is also, in Hirsch's formulation, "re-authoring" it. But to rewrite a text is not to reread it, and if the author is indeed rewriting, then the text he is now producing is, as we have noted, not the same as the earlier one. The fact that he meant something different in the earlier text, and that he knows that he meant something different, is irrelevant

---

5. As we noted in "Against Theory," the possibility of preferring one's mistake is irrelevant to the problem of interpretive method; such a preference "might affect what one does *with* an interpretation, but it has no effect on how one *gets* an interpretation" (p. 18 n.7).

to what he means now—just as what he means now is irrelevant to what he meant then.

All Hirsch's example shows is that you can either read a text or write one, and that the choice between interpreting the intention of the text's composer and "postulating" the intention of some other author is a choice between reading and writing. Of course, Hirsch is right to think that we might choose to re-author a poem instead of interpret it, but this possibility has nothing to do with the practice of interpretation. The distinction between reading and writing is clearly not a distinction between two methods of reading, one of them faithful to the historical author's intention and the other not.

In our view, the object of all reading is always the historical author's intention, even if the historical author is the universal muse. That's why we don't think it makes sense to *choose* historical intention—and why we don't think it's possible to choose any other kind of intention. Hence the formalist understanding of the consequences of "Against Theory" is as mistaken as Hirsch's and, interestingly enough, mistaken in the same way. Not only do Hirsch and Dowling both think that "Against Theory" allows a distinction between intention as a *"purely formal"* requirement in interpretation and the intention of a historical author (Dowling, p. 93)—they both think that "Against Theory" endorses a preference for the former. But where Hirsch regrets that the "most probable effect" of "Against Theory" will be "to foster the comforting idea that there's no point in pursuing historical scholarship," Dowling is pleased to find us providing a justification for a "formalist program of objective interpretation" (Dowling, p. 93).

In Dowling's perceptive account of American formalism, the New Critical rejection of intention was never absolute. Instead of dismissing intention, the New Critics recognized that "meaning must always *in purely formal terms* involve intention" and that "where there is an intention there must always be an intender" (Dowling, p. 93). The New Critics only meant to exclude "authorial intention" (Dowling, p. 94); in Hirsch's terms, they chose a "postulated" intention over a historical one. For Dowling, this choice means that interpretation begins "by positing something like the internal voice or speaker of formalist theory" (Dowling, p. 93).

Dowling is right to think that nothing in "Against Theory" rules out positing an internal speaker in the sense of a persona or narrator. But to posit such an internal speaker is not, as he thinks, to rule out an external authorial intention; it is simply to interpret that intention—in this case, an intention to produce an internal speaker. If, on the other hand, positing an internal speaker means *replacing* the authorial intention with some other intention, then this simply becomes another case of rewriting and is no longer interpretation at all. Thus, what Dowling calls the "formalist program of interpretation" is just like everyone else's program of interpretation: it consists in the attempt (sometimes successful, sometimes not) to find out what the historical author meant.[6]

To insist, as we do, that the object of interpretation is always a historical intention is, once again, not to justify or even to recommend the pursuit of historical scholarship. Textual editors, historical scholars, New Critical explicators, and everyone else—from the standpoint of intention—are all doing the same thing. Since it provides no help in choosing among critical procedures, the idea of intention is methodologically useless.

3. The Profession

Even if it is granted that our account of interpretation can have no methodological consequences, two of our critics are distressed by the possible effect of "Against Theory" on the profession of literary criticism. According to Crewe, "Against Theory," encouraging a "defensive adherence to the procedures and values of the guild," not only promotes "business as usual" but amounts to a "petty theodicy of the guild" (Crewe, pp. 58, 60). For O'Hara, the "practical effect" of "Against Theory" is not so much to promote "business as usual" as to restore it to the way it was, leaving "the field open to the long-established and well-heeled, native American, fly-by-the-seat-of-one's-pants critical pragmatists and know-nothings, who have been waiting in the wings ever since the late sixties for such boring annoyances as critical theory, feminism, affirmative action programs, and so forth to disappear" (O'Hara, p. 37). Where Crewe thinks we are serving an "emergent ideology" of professionalism (Crewe, p. 54), O'Hara thinks we are inhibiting the growth of the profession: just as theorists are beginning to realize "the first fruits of their labors to institutionalize theory as a sub-

6. William Dowling's acknowledgment of an internal speaker's intention seems to modify the usual formalist insistence on the intrinsic meaningfulness of linguistic forms. But his discussion of the sentence "I was whipped" makes it clear that the modification is only apparent. According to Dowling, "I was whipped" can mean many things but not just anything, and this fact "shows that (1) certain rules of determinacy are already in force and (2) that an account of meaning *already* assumes that an intention . . . is also present" (Dowling, p. 93). But if "I was whipped" has no meaning in itself—if, in other words, it has meaning only as the expression of someone's intention—why can't it be used to mean anything at all? The antiformalist point of "Against Theory" is to insist that anything can be used to mean anything or, as Crewe rightly puts it, "quite radically to deny that the forms of language possess any defining power." Crewe objects that such a position ignores the importance of "convention," betraying "an obliviousness of the socially constructed and consensual nature of linguistic significance" (Crewe, p. 61). But to insist on the primacy of intention is not to deny the importance of convention; it is only to point out that conventions don't even count as conventions unless they are intended.

discipline within the critical profession," along comes our attempt to take theory away, or at least make it "less attractive" as a "career option" (O'Hara, pp. 32, 37).[7]

Our remarks on method may already suggest why we don't think these professional consequences follow from our arguments any more than the methodological ones did. Just as our argument against theory is compatible with (and indifferent to) all modes of critical practice, it is also compatible with and indifferent to all ways of organizing that practice. Nothing in "Against Theory" tells you whether programs in women's studies are a good thing, whether teachers should be tenured, or whether graduate programs should be maintained or cut back in response to the current job crisis. This is not to deny that we ourselves have views on these questions, just as we have views on the relative merits of historical scholarship and close reading; it is only to insist that such views have no relation to our account of interpretation.

Not only is "Against Theory" indifferent to particular ways of *organizing* the profession; it is indifferent to the *existence* of the profession. A certain reading of "Against Theory" might take our insistence on the inescapability of practice as a way of preserving the profession by purging it of theory. Thus Crewe understands our attack on theory as the expression of a kind of professional populism: an attempt to defend the traditional practices of the institution against a new "tool of institutional domination" (Crewe, p. 56). Crewe's point, of course, is that in defending practice we are merely substituting one form of institutional domination for another.

But in focusing on institutional politics, Crewe has missed our point. Crewe understands our account of interpretation as a description of the interpretive practice of a certain institution. But our account of interpretation, if true, describes the way interpretation *always* works, irrespective of its relation to any institution. Any interpreter of any utterance or text, within the institution of professional literary criticism or not, is, if we are right, attempting to understand the author's intention. The profession of literary criticism could utterly disappear, and this event would in no way alter the fact that texts mean what their authors intend.

If our arguments are true, they can have only one consequence (the single consequence they claim to have); theory should stop. If accepted, our arguments would indeed eliminate the "career option" of writing and teaching theory. Perhaps newly unemployed theorists could be retrained to teach courses in the history of theory. In fact, however, we don't think that theory is likely to end any time soon. But we do think that theory, like our arguments against it, will continue to have no consequences for the practice of literary criticism.

7. Bizarre as it sounds, Daniel O'Hara's careerist fantasy is more plausible than Crewe's assumption that theory subjects the profession to "fundamental questioning."

Consequences

Stanley Fish

Nothing I wrote in *Is There a Text in This Class?* has provoked more opposition or consternation than my (negative) claim that the argument of the book has no consequences for the practice of literary criticism.[1] To many it seemed counterintuitive to maintain (as I did) that an argument in theory could leave untouched the practice it considers: After all, isn't the very point of theory to throw light on or reform or guide practice? In answer to this question, I want to say, first, that this is certainly theory's claim—so much so that independently of the claim there is no reason to think of it as a separate activity—and, second, that the claim is unsupportable. Here, I am in agreement with Steven Knapp and Walter Benn Michaels, who are almost alone in agreeing with me and who fault me not for making the "no consequences" argument but for occasionally falling away from it. Those who dislike *Is There a Text in This Class?* tend to dislike "Against Theory" even more, and it is part of my purpose here to account for the hostility to both pieces. But since the issues at stake are fundamental, it is incumbent to begin at the beginning with a discussion of what theory is and is not.

"Against Theory" opens with a straightforward (if compressed) definition: "By 'theory' we mean a special project in literary criticism: the attempt to govern interpretations of particular texts by appealing to an account of interpretation in general" (p. 11). In the second sentence the authors declare that this definition of theory excludes much that has been thought to fall under its rubric and especially excludes projects of

Reprinted from the March 1985 issue of *Critical Inquiry*.

a general nature "such as narratology, stylistics, and prosody" (p. 11).
On first blush this exclusion seems arbitrary and appears to be vulnerable
to the charge (made by several respondents) that by defining theory so
narrowly Knapp and Michaels at once assure the impregnability of their
thesis and render it trivial. I believe, on the contrary, that the definition
is correct and that, moreover, it is a reformulation of a familiar and even
uncontroversial distinction. In E. D. Hirsch's work, for example, we meet
it as a distinction between general and local hermeneutics. "Local hermeneutics," Hirsch explains,

> consists of rules of thumb rather than rules. . . . Local hermeneutics
> can . . . provide models and methods that are reliable most of the
> time. General hermeneutics lays claim to principles that hold true
> all of the time. . . . That is why general hermeneutics is, so far, the
> only aspect of interpretation that has earned the right to be named
> a "theory."[2]

By "general hermeneutics," Hirsch means a procedure whose steps, if
they are faithfully and strictly followed, will "always yield correct results";[3]
"local hermeneutics," on the other hand, are calculations of probability
based on an insider's knowledge of what is likely to be successful in a
particular field of practice. When Cicero advises that in cases where a
client's character is an issue a lawyer should attribute a bad reputation
to "the envy of a few people, or back biting, or false opinion" or, failing
that, argue that "the defendant's life and character are not under investigation, but only the crime of which he is accused," he is presenting
and urging a local hermeneutics. But when Raoul Berger insists that the
meaning of the Constitution can be determined only by determining the
intentions of the framers, he is presenting and urging a general hermeneutics.[4] In one case, the practitioner is being told "In a situation like
this, here are some of the things you can do," where it is left to the agent
to determine whether or not he has encountered a situation "like this"
and which of the possible courses of action is relevant. In the other case,
the practitioner is being told "When you want to know the truth or
discover the meaning, do this," where "this" is a set of wholly explicit
instructions that leaves no room for interpretive decisions by the agent.
In one case, the practitioner is being given a "rule of thumb," something

---

Stanley Fish is the William Kenan, Jr., Professor of English and the
Humanities at the Johns Hopkins University. The present essay is the
concluding chapter of *Change* (forthcoming, 1985).

that would in certain circumstances be a good thing to try if you want to succeed in the game; in the other, he is being given a rule, something that is necessary to do if you want to be right, where "being right" is not a matter of being in tune with the temporary and shifting norms of a context but of having adhered to the dictates of an abiding and general rationality. A rule is formalizable: it can be programmed on a computer and, therefore, can be followed by anyone who has been equipped with explicit (noncircular) definitions and equally explicit directions for carrying out a procedure. A rule of thumb, on the other hand, cannot be formalized, because the conditions of its application vary with the contextual circumstances of an ongoing practice; as those circumstances change, the very meaning of the rule (the instructions it is understood to give) changes too, at least for someone sufficiently inside the practice to be sensitive to its shifting demands. To put it another way, the rule-of-thumb reader begins with a knowledge of the outcome he desires, and it is within such knowledge that the rule assumes a shape, becomes readable; the rule follower, in contrast, defers to the self-declaring shape of the rule, which then generates the correct outcome independently of his judgment. The model for the "true" rule and, therefore, for theory is mathematics, for as John Lyons points out, if two people apply the rules of mathematics and come up with different results, we can be sure that one of them is mistaken, that is, has misapplied the rules.[5]

Lyons turns to the analogy from mathematics in the course of an explication of Chomskian linguistics, and the Chomsky project provides an excellent example of what a model of the formal, or rule-governed, type would be like. The Chomskian revolution, as Jerrold Katz and Thomas Bever have written, involved "the shift from a conception of grammar as cataloguing the data of a corpus to a conception of grammar as explicating the internalized rules underlying the speaker's ability to produce and understand sentences."[6] Basically this is a turn from an empirical activity—the deriving of grammatical rules from a finite body of observed sentences—to a rational activity—the discovery of a set of constraints which, rather than being generalizations from observed behavior, are explanatory of that behavior in the sense that they are what make it possible. These constraints are not acquired through experience (education, historical conditioning, local habits) but are innate; experience serves only to actualize or "trigger" them. They have their source not in culture but in nature, and therefore they are *abstract* (without empirical content), *general* (not to be identified with any particular race, location, or historical period but with the species), and *invariant* (do not differ from language to language). As a system of rules, they are "independent of the features of the actual world and thus hold in any possible one" ("FRE," p. 40).

It follows that any attempt to model these constraints—to construct a device that will replicate their operations—must be equally independent in all these ways, that is, it must be formal, abstract, general, and invariant.

It is Chomsky's project to construct such a device, a model of an innate human ability, a "competence model" which reflects the timeless and contextless workings of an abiding formalism, as opposed to a "performance model" which would reflect the empirical and contingent regularities of the behavior of some particular linguistic community. Once constructed, a competence model would function in the manner of a "mechanical computation" ("FRE," p. 38); that is, to "apply" it would be to set in motion a self-executing machine or calculus that would assign, without any interpretive activity on the part of the applier, the same description to a sentence that would be assigned by "an ideal speaker-listener, in a completely homogeneous speech-community, who knows its language perfectly."[7] If such a speaker were presented with the sentence "He danced his did," he would reject it as ungrammatical or irregular or deviant. Accordingly, a grammar modeled on his ability (or intuition) would refuse to assign the sentence a description—the generative device would find itself blocked by an item that violated its rules. If such a speaker were presented with the sentence "Flying planes can be dangerous," he would recognize it as ambiguous; accordingly, a generative grammar would assign the sentence not one but two structural (or "deep") descriptions. And if such a speaker were presented with the pair of sentences "John hit the ball" and "The ball was hit by John," he would recognize them as being synonymous, and, accordingly, the generative grammar would assign them a single structural description.

It is important to realize that this ideal speaker and the grammar modeled on his competence would perform their tasks without taking into account the circumstances of a sentence's production, or the beliefs of the speaker and hearer, or the idiomatic patterns of a particular community.[8] The speaker who knows the language of his community "perfectly" in Chomsky's idealization knows that system independently of its actualization in real-life situations: that knowledge is his competence, and the grammar that captures it divides strings in a language "into the well-formed and the ill-formed just on the basis of their syntactic structure, without reference to the way things are in the world, what speakers, hearers, or anyone else believe, etc." ("FRE," p. 31). That is why, as Judith Greene puts it, "the only real test . . . of a grammar is to devise a set of formal rules which, if fed to a computer operating with no prior knowledge of the language, would still be capable of generating only correct grammatical sentences."[9]

This is precisely the goal of Chomskian theory—the construction of "a system of rules that in some explicit and well-defined way assigns structural descriptions to sentences," where "explicit" means mechanical or algorithmic and the assigning is done not by the agent but by the system (*ATS*, p. 8). Needless to say, there has been much dispute concerning the possibility (and even desirability) of achieving that goal, and there have been many challenges to the basic distinctions (between competence and performance, between grammaticality and acceptability, between syntax and semantics, between grammatical knowledge and the knowledge of the world) that permit the goal, first, to be formulated and, then, to guide a program of research. But putting aside the merits of the Chomsky program and the question of whether it could ever succeed, the point I want to make here is that as a program it is theoretical and can stand as a fully developed example of what Knapp and Michaels mean when they say that theory is a *special* project and what Hirsch means when he insists that only such a project—a general hermeneutics—"has earned the right to be named a 'theory.'" The Chomsky project is theoretical because what it seeks is a method, a recipe with premeasured ingredients which when ordered and combined according to absolutely explicit instructions— instructions that "[do] not rely on the intelligence of the understanding reader" (*ATS*, p. 4)—will produce the desired result. In linguistics that result would be the assigning of correct descriptions to sentences; in literary studies the result would be the assigning of valid interpretations to works of literature. In both cases (and in any other that could be imagined), the practitioner gives himself over to the theoretical machine, surrenders his judgment to it, in order to reach conclusions that in no way depend on his education, or point of view, or cultural situation, conclusions that can then be checked by anyone who similarly binds himself to those rules and carries out their instructions.

Thus understood, theory can be seen as an effort to govern practice in two senses: (1) it is an attempt to *guide* practice from a position above or outside it (see pp. 11 and 30), and (2) it is an attempt to *reform* practice by neutralizing interest, by substituting for the parochial perspective of some local or partisan point of view the perspective of a general rationality to which the individual subordinates his contextually conditioned opinions and beliefs. (Not incidentally, this is the claim and the dream of Baconian method, of which so many modern theoretical projects are heirs.) Only if this substitution is accomplished will interpretation be principled, that is, impelled by formal and universal rules that apply always and everywhere rather than by rules of thumb that reflect the contingent practices of particular communities.

The argument *against* theory is simply that this substitution of the general for the local has never been and will never be achieved. Theory is an impossible project which will never succeed. It will never succeed simply because the primary data and formal laws necessary to its success will always be spied or picked out from within the contextual circumstances of which they are supposedly independent. The objective facts and rules of calculation that are to ground interpretation and render it principled are themselves interpretive products: they are, therefore, always and already contaminated by the interested judgments they claim to transcend.

The contingencies that are to be excluded in favor of the invariant constitute the field within which what will (for a time) be termed the invariant emerges.

Once again, a ready example offers itself in the history of Chomskian linguistics. In order to get started, Chomsky must exclude from his "absolute formulations . . . any factor that should be considered as a matter of performance rather than competence." He does this, as Katz and Bever observe, "by simply considering the former [performance] as something to be abstracted away from, the way the physicist excludes friction, air resistance, and so on from the formulation of mechanical laws" ("FRE," p. 21). This act of abstracting-away-from must of course begin with data, and in this case the data are (or are supposed to be) sentences that depend for their interpretation not on performance factors—on the knowledge of a speaker's beliefs or of particular customs or conventions—but on the rules of grammar.[10] The trick then is to think of sentences that would be heard in the same way by all competent speakers no matter what their educational experience, or class membership, or partisan affiliation, or special knowledge, sentences which, invariant across contexts, could form the basis of an acontextual and formal description of the language and its rules.

The trouble is that there are no such sentences. As I have argued elsewhere, even to think of a sentence is to have already assumed the conditions both of its production and its intelligibility—conditions that include a speaker, with an intention and a purpose, in a situation.[11] To be sure, there are sentences which, when presented, seem to be intelligible in isolation, independently of any contextual setting. This simply means however, that the context is so established, so deeply assumed, that it is invisible to the observer—he does not realize that what appears to him to be immediately obvious and readable is a function of its being in place. It follows, then, that any rules arrived at by abstracting away from such sentences will be rules only within the silent or deep context that allowed them to emerge and become describable. Rather than being distinct from circumstantial (and therefore variable) conditions, linguistic knowledge is unthinkable apart from these circumstances. Linguistic knowledge is contextual rather than abstract, local rather than general, dynamic rather than invariant; every rule is a rule of thumb; every competence grammar is a performance grammar in disguise.[12]

This then is why theory will never succeed: it cannot help but borrow its terms and its content from that which it claims to transcend, the mutable world of practice, belief, assumptions, point of view, and so forth. And, by definition, something that cannot succeed cannot have consequences, cannot achieve the goals it has set for itself by being or claiming to be theory, the goals of guiding and/or reforming practice. Theory cannot guide practice because its rules and procedures are no more than generalizations from practice's history (and from only a small piece of that history), and theory cannot reform practice because, rather than neutralizing interest, it begins and ends in interest and raises the imperatives of interest—of some local, particular, partisan project—to the status of universals.

Thus far I have been talking about "foundationalist" theory (what Knapp and Michaels call "positive theory"), theory that promises to put our calculations and determinations on a firmer footing than can be provided by mere belief or unjustified practice. In recent years, however, the focus of attention has been more on "antifoundationalist" theory (what Knapp and Michaels call "negative theory"), on arguments whose force it is precisely to deny the possibility (and even the intelligibility) of what foundationalist theory promises. Antifoundationalist theory is sometimes Kuhnian, sometimes Derridean, sometimes pragmatist, sometimes Marxist, sometimes anarchist, but it is always historicist; that is, its strategy is always the one I have pursued in the previous paragraphs, namely, to demonstrate that the norms and standards and rules that foundationalist theory would oppose to history, convention, and local practice are in every instance a function or extension of history, convention, and local practice. As Richard Rorty puts it: "There are no essences anywhere in the area. There is no wholesale, epistemological way to direct, or criticize or underwrite the course of inquiry. . . . It is the vocabulary of practice rather than of theory . . . in which one can say something useful about truth."[13] (Notice that this does not mean that a notion like "truth" ceases to be operative, only that it will always have reference to a moment in the history of inquiry rather than to some God or material objectivity or invariant calculus that underwrites all of our inquiries.)

The fact that there are two kinds of theory (or, rather, theoretical discourse—antifoundationalism really isn't a theory at all; it is an argument against the possibility of theory) complicates the question of consequences, although in the end the relationship of both kinds of theory to the question turns out to be the same. As we have seen, those who believe in the consequences of foundationalist theory are possessed by a hope— let us call it "theory hope"—the hope that our claims to knowledge can be "justified on the basis of some objective method of assessing such claims" rather than on the basis of the individual beliefs that have been derived from the accidents of education and experience.[14] Antifoundationalist theory tells us that no such justification will ever be available and that therefore there is no way of testing our beliefs against something whose source is not also a belief. As we shall see, antifoundationalism comes with its own version of "theory hope," but the emotion its arguments more often provoke is "theory fear," the fear that those who have been persuaded by such arguments will abandon principled inquiry and go their unconstrained way in response to the dictates of fashion, opinion, or whim. Expressions of theory fear abound (one can find them now even in daily newspapers and popular magazines), and in their more dramatic forms they approach the status of prophecies of doom. Here, for example, is Israel Scheffler's view of what will happen if we are persuaded by the writings of Thomas Kuhn:

> Independent and public controls are no more, communication has failed, the common universe of things is a delusion, reality itself is made . . . rather than discovered. . . . In place of a community of rational men following objective procedures in the pursuit of truth, we have a set of isolated monads, within each of which belief forms without systematic constraints.[15]

For Scheffler (and many others) the consequences of antifoundationalist theory are disastrous and amount to the loss of everything we associate with rational inquiry: public and shared standards, criteria for preferring one reading of a text or of the world to another, checks against irresponsibility, and so on. But this follows only if antifoundationalism is an argument for unbridled subjectivity, for the absence of constraints on the individual; whereas, in fact, it is an argument for the situated subject, for the individual who is always constrained by the local or community standards and criteria of which his judgment is an extension. Thus the lesson of antifoundationalism is not only that external and independent guides will never be found but that it is unnecessary to seek them, because you will always be guided by the rules or rules of thumb that are the content of any settled practice, by the assumed definitions, distinctions, criteria of evidence, measures of adequacy, and such, which not only define the practice but structure the understanding of the agent who thinks of himself as a "competent member." That agent cannot distance himself from these rules, because it is only within them that he can think about alternative courses of action or, indeed, think at all. Thus antifoundationalism cannot possibly have the consequences Scheffler fears; for, rather than unmooring the subject, it reveals the subject to be always and already tethered to the contextual setting that constitutes him and enables his "rational" acts.

Neither can antifoundationalism have the consequences for which some of its proponents *hope,* the consequences of freeing us from the hold of unwarranted absolutes so that we may more flexibly pursue the goals of human flourishing or liberal conversation. The reasoning behind this hope is that since we now know that our convictions about truth and factuality have not been imposed on us by the world, or imprinted in our brains, but are derived from the practices of ideologically motivated communities, we can set them aside in favor of convictions that we choose freely. But this is simply to imagine the moment of unconstrained choice from the other direction, as a goal rather than as an abyss. Antifoundationalist fear and antifoundationalist hope turn out to differ only in emphasis. Those who express the one are concerned lest we kick ourselves loose from constraints; those who profess the other look forward to finally being able to do so. Both make the mistake of thinking that antifoundationalism, by demonstrating the contextual source of conviction, cuts the ground out from under conviction—it is just that, for one party, this is the good news and, for the other, it is the news that chaos has come again. But, in fact, antifoundationalism says nothing about what we can now do or not do; it is an account of what we have always been doing and cannot help but do (no matter what our views on epistemology)— act in accordance with the standards and norms that are the content of our beliefs and, therefore, the very structure of our consciousness. The fact that we now have a new explanation of how we got our beliefs— the fact, in short, that we now have a new belief—does not free us from our other beliefs or cause us to doubt them. I may now be convinced that what I think about *Paradise Lost* is a function of my education, professional training, the history of Milton studies, and so on, but that conviction does not lead me to think something else about *Paradise Lost* or to lose confidence in what I think. These consequences would follow only if I also believed in the possibility of a method independent of belief by which the truth about *Paradise Lost* could be determined; but if I believed that, I wouldn't be an antifoundationalist at all. In short, the theory hope expressed by some antifoundationalists is incoherent within the antifoundationalist perspective, since it assumes, in its dream of beginning anew, everything that antifoundationalism rejects.

Of course it could be the case that if I were shown that some of my convictions (about Milton or anything else) could be traced to sources in sets of assumptions or points of view I found distressing, I might be moved either to alter those convictions or reexamine my sense of what is and is not distressing. This, however, would be a quite specific reconsideration provoked by a perceived inconsistency in my beliefs (and it would have to be an inconsistency that struck me as intolerable), not a general reconsideration of my beliefs in the face of a belief about their source. To be sure, such a general reconsideration would be possible if the source to which I had come to attribute them was deemed by me to be discreditable (hallucinatory drugs, political indoctrination)—although even then I could still decide that I was sticking with what I now knew no matter where it came from—but human history could not be that kind of discreditable source for me as an antifoundationalist, since antifoundationalism teaches (and teaches without regret or nostalgia) that human history is the context within which we know. To put it another way, an antifoundationalist (like anyone else) can always reject something because its source has been shown to be some piece of human history he finds reprehensible, but an antifoundationalist cannot (without at that moment becoming a foundationalist) reject something simply because its source has been shown to be human history as opposed to something independent of it.

All of which is to say again what I have been saying all along: theory has no consequences. Foundationalist theory has no consequences because its project cannot succeed, and antifoundationalist theory has no consequences because, as a belief about how we got our beliefs, it leaves untouched (at least in principle) the beliefs of whose history it is an explanation. The case seems open-and-shut, but I am aware that many will maintain that theory *must* have consequences. It is to their objections and arguments that I now turn.

The first objection has already been disposed of, at least implicitly. It is Adena Rosmarin's objection and amounts to asking Why restrict theory either to foundationalist attempts to ground practice by some Archimedean principle or to antifoundationalist demonstrations that all such attempts will necessarily fail? Why exclude from the category "theory" much that has always been regarded as theory—works like W. J. Harvey's *Character in the Novel,* or Barbara Herrnstein Smith's *Poetic Closure,* or William Empson's *Seven Types of Ambiguity*—works whose claims are general and extend beyond the interpretation of specific texts to the uncovering of regularities that are common to a great many texts? The answer is that the regularities thus uncovered, rather than standing apart from practice and constituting an abstract picture of its possibilities, would be derived from practice and constitute a report on its current shape or on the shape it once had in an earlier period. It is possible to think of these regularities as rules, but they would be neither invariant nor predictive since they would be drawn from a finite corpus of data and would hold (if they did hold) only for that corpus; each time history brought forward new instances, it would be necessary to rewrite the "rules," that is, re-characterize the regularities. In Chomsky's terms, the result would be a succession of performance grammars, grammars that reflect the shifting and contingent conditions of a community's practice rather than capture the laws that constrain what the members of a community can possibly do. The result, in short, would be *empirical generalizations* rather than a general hermeneutics.

Still, one might ask, Why not call such generalizations "theory"? Of course, there is nothing to prevent us from doing so, but the effect of such a liberal definition would be to blur the distinction between theory and everything that is not theory, so that, for example, essays on the functions of prefaces in Renaissance drama would be theory, and books on the pastoral would be theory, and studies of Renaissance self-fashioning or self-consuming artifacts would be theory. One is tempted to call such efforts theory in part because they often serve as models for subsequent work: one could study self-fashioning in the eighteenth century or self-consuming artifacts as a feature of modernism. Such activities, though, would be instances not of following a theory but of extending a practice, of employing a set of heuristic questions, or a thematics, or a trenchant distinction in such a way as to produce a new or at least novel description of familiar material. Much of what is done in literary studies and elsewhere conforms to this pattern. If we like, we can always call such imitations of a powerful practice "theory," but nothing whatsoever will have been gained, and we will have lost any sense that theory is special. After all, it is only if theory is special that the question of its consequences is in any way urgent. In other words, the consequentiality of theory goes without saying and is, therefore, totally uninteresting if *everything* is theory.

And yet the argument that everything is theory is sometimes put forward in *support* of theory's special status. Those who make this argument think it follows from the chief lesson of antifoundationalism, the lesson that there are no unmediated facts nor any neutral perception and that everything we know and see is known and seen under a description or as a function of some paradigm. The conclusion drawn from this lesson is that every practice presupposes a structure of assumptions within which it is intelligible—there is no such thing as *simply* acting—and the conclusion drawn from that conclusion is that every practice is underwritten by a theory. The first conclusion seems to me to be correct—any practice one engages in is conceivable only in relation to some belief or set of beliefs— but the second conclusion is, I think, false, because beliefs are not theories. A theory is a special achievement of consciousness; a belief is a prerequisite for being conscious at all. Beliefs are not what you think *about* but what you think *with*, and it is within the space provided by their articulations that mental activity—including the activity of theorizing—goes on. Theories are something you can have—you can wield them and hold them at a distance; beliefs have *you*, in the sense that there can be no distance between them and the acts they enable. In order to make even the simplest of assertions or perform the most elementary action, I must already be proceeding in the context of innumerable beliefs which cannot be the object of my attention, because they are the content of my attention: beliefs on the order of the identity of persons, the existence of animate and inanimate entities, the stability of objects, in addition to the countless beliefs that underwrite the possibility and intelligibility of events in my local culture—beliefs that give me, without reflection, a world populated by streets, sidewalks, telephone poles, restaurants, figures of authority and figures of fun, worthy and unworthy tasks, achievable and unachievable goals, and so on. The description of what assumptions must already be in place for me to enter an elevator, or stand in line in a supermarket, or ask for the check in a restaurant would fill volumes, volumes that would themselves be intelligible only within a set of assumptions they in turn did not contain. Do these volumes—and the volumes that would be necessary to their description—constitute a theory? Am I following or enacting a theory when I stop for a red light, or use my American Express card, or rise to speak at a conference? Are you now furiously theorizing as you sit reading what I have to say? And if you are persuaded by me to alter your understanding of what is and is not a theory, is your new definition of theory a new theory of theory? Clearly it is possible to answer yes to all these questions, but just as clearly that answer will render the notion "theory" *and* the issue of its consequences trivial by making "theory" the name for ordinary, contingent, unpredictable, everyday behavior.

Now it may be easy enough to see the absurdity of giving the label "theoretical" to everyday actions that follow from the first or ground-level beliefs that give us our world. The difficulty arises with actions that seem more momentous and are attached to large questions of policy and morality; such actions, we tend to feel, must follow from something more "considered" than a mere belief, must follow, rather, from a theory. Thus, for example, consider the case of two legislators who must vote on a fair housing bill: one is committed to the protection of individual freedom and insists that it trump all competing considerations; the other is some kind of utilitarian and is committed to the greatest good for the greatest number. Isn't it accurate to say that these two hold different theories and that their respective theories will lead them to cast different votes — the first, against, and the second, in favor of, fair housing? Well, first, it is not at all certain that the actions of the two are predictable on the basis of what we are for now calling their "theories." A utilitarian may well think that, in the long run, the greatest number will reap the greatest good if property rights are given more weight than access rights; a libertarian could well decide that access rights are more crucial to the promotion of individual freedom and choice than property rights. In short, nothing particular follows from the fact that the two agents in my example would, if asked, declare themselves adherents of different theories. But would they even be theories? I would say not. Someone who declares himself committed to the promotion of individual freedom does not have a theory; he has a belief. He believes that something is more important than something else—and if you were to inquire into the grounds of his belief, you would discover not a theory but other beliefs that at once support and are supported by the belief to which he is currently testifying. Now, to be sure, these clustered beliefs affect behavior—not because they are consulted when a problem presents itself, however, but because it is within the world they deliver that the problem and its possible solutions take shape. To put it another way, when one acts on the basis of a belief, one is just engaged in reasoning, not in theoretical reasoning, and it makes no difference whether the belief is so deep as to be invisible or is invoked within a highly dramatic, even spectacular, situation. The sequence "I believe in the promotion of individual freedom, and therefore I will vote in this rather than in that way" is not different in kind from the sequence "I believe in the solidity of matter and therefore I will open the door rather than attempt to walk through the walls." It seems curious to call the reasoning (if that is the word) in the second sequence "theoretical," and I am saying that it would be no less curious to give that name to the reasoning in the first. The fact that someone has a very general, even philosophical, belief—a belief concerning recognizably "big" issues—does not mean that he has a theory; it just means that he has a very general belief. If someone wants to say that his very general belief has a consequential (although not predictable) relationship to his action, I am certainly not going to argue, since to say that is to say what I said at the beginning of this section: it is belief and not theory that underwrites action.

It is simply a mistake, then, to think that someone who identifies himself as a believer in individual freedom or in the greatest good for the greatest number has declared his allegiance to a theory. But there are instances in which it is indeed proper to say that someone who takes this rather than that position is opting for this rather than that theory, and in those instances the question of the consequences of theory is once again alive. Here, a recent essay by Thomas Grey of the Stanford Law School provides a useful example. Grey is concerned with the consequences for the judicial process of two theories of constitutional interpretation. Those who hold the first theory he calls "textualists," and in their view "judges should get operative norms only from the text," that is, from the Constitution. Those who hold the other theory he calls "supplementers," and in their view "judges may find supplemental norms through [the] interpretation of text analogs" such as previous judicial decisions or background social phenomena.[16] I regard these two positions as theoretical because they amount to alternative sets of instructions for reaching correct or valid interpretive conclusions. Someone who says "I am committed to promoting individual freedom" still has the task, in every situation, of deciding which among the alternative courses of action will further his ends. But a judge who says "I get my operative norms only from the text" knows exactly what to do in every situation: he looks to the text and restricts himself to the norms he finds there. On the other side, his "supplementalist" opponent also knows what to do: he looks for norms not only in the text but in a number of other, authorized, places. Grey forthrightly identifies himself as a supplementer, arguing that if lawyers and judges come to think of themselves as supplementers rather than textualists, as one kind of theorist rather than as another, they "will thereby be marginally more free than they otherwise would be to infuse into constitutional law their current interpretations of our society's values."

For Grey, then, the consequences of theory are real and important. It seems obvious to him that (1) if two judges, one a textualist and the other a supplementer, were presented with the same case they would decide it differently, and (2) the differences in their decisions would be a function of the differences in their theories. This assumes, however, that the two theories give instructions that it is possible to follow and that someone *could* first identify the norms encoded in the text and then choose either to abide by them or to supplement them. But as Grey himself acknowledges, interpretation is not a two-stage process in which the interpreter first picks out a "context-independent semantic meaning" and then, if he chooses, consults this or that context; rather, it is within some or other context—of assumptions, concerns, priorities, expectations—that what an interpreter sees as the "semantic meaning" emerges, and therefore he is never in the position of being able to focus on that meaning independently of background or "supplemental" considerations. The semantic meaning of the text does not announce itself; it must be decided upon, that is, interpreted. Since this is also true of contexts—they too must be construed—the distinction between text and context is impossible to maintain and cannot be the basis of demarcating alternative theories with their attendant consequences. In short, no text reads itself, and anything you decide to take into account—any supplement—is a text; therefore interpreters of the Constitution are always and *necessarily* both textualists and supplementers, and the only argument between them is an argument over which text it is that is going to be read or, if you prefer, which set of background conditions will be specified as the text. Those arguments have substance, and on many occasions their outcomes will have consequences, but they will not be the consequences of having followed one or the other of these two theories because, while they truly are theories, they cannot be followed. If the two judges in our example did in fact happen to reach different decisions about the same case, it would not be because they have different theories of interpretation but because they interpret from within different sets of priorities or concerns, that is, from within different sets of beliefs. It is entirely possible, moreover, that despite the declared differences in theoretical allegiance, the two could reach exactly the same decision whenever the text to which the one has confined himself is perspicuous against the same set of supplemental concerns or perspectives that forms the other's text.

And yet it would be too much to say that declarations of theoretical allegiances—even allegiances to theories that cannot be made operative—are inconsequential. As Grey notes, such declarations have a political force: "Most lawyers," he points out, "share with the public a 'pre-realist' consensus that in doing judicial review, judges should generate their decisive norms by constitutional interpretation only." In short, there is a consensus that they should be textualists; therefore, Grey contends, "For me to call my views 'noninterpretive' [supplementalist] will obviously not improve my chances of winning the argument." Now one could dismiss this as a piece of cynical advice ("Call yourself a textualist no matter how you proceed"), but it seems to me to point to a significant truth: rather than dictating or generating arguments, theoretical positions are parts of arguments and are often invoked because of a perceived connection between them and certain political and ideological stands. That is, given a certain set of political circumstances, one or another theory will be a component in this or that agenda or program. So, for example, in a struggle for power between the judiciary and the legislature, one party

120   Stanley Fish

may gravitate "naturally"—that is, in terms of its current goals—toward
one theory while the other party—just as naturally and just as politically—
identifies itself with the opposite theory. Moreover, in the course of a
generation or two, the identifications may be reversed, as new circumstances
find the onetime textualists now calling themselves supplementers (or
legal realists, or "noninterpretivists") and vice versa. In short, declaring
a theoretical allegiance will often be consequential—not, however, because
the declaration dictates a course of action but because a course of action
already in full flower appropriates it and gives it significance.

Thus we see that even when something is a theory and is consequential—in the sense that espousing it counts for something—it is not
consequential in the way theorists claim. Indeed, on the evidence of the
examples we have so far considered, the possible relationships between
theories and consequences reduce to three: either (1) it *is* a theory but
has no consequences because, as a set of directions purged of interest
and independent of presuppositions, it cannot be implemented, or (2)
it has consequences but is not a theory—rather, it is a belief or a conviction,
as in the case of the promotion of individual freedom, or (3) it is a theory
and does have consequences, but they are political rather than theoretical,
as when, for very good practical reasons, somebody calls himself a textualist
or a supplementer.

Nevertheless there still is a position to which a "consequentialist"
might retreat: perhaps theory, strictly speaking, is an impossible project
that could never succeed, and perhaps beliefs and assumptions, while
consequential, are not theories—but, Isn't the foregrounding of beliefs
and assumptions "theory"?—and, Doesn't the foregrounding of beliefs
and assumptions make us more aware of them?—and, Isn't that a consequence, and one which will itself have consequences? In short, theory
may be just an activity within practice, but—as this position would have
it—Isn't it a special *kind* of activity? This claim has two versions, one
weak and one strong. The strong version is untenable because it reinvents
foundationalism, and the weak version is so weak that to grant it is to
have granted nothing at all. The strong claim reinvents foundationalism
because it imagines a position from which our beliefs can be scrutinized;
that is, it imagines a position outside belief, the transcendental position
assumed and sought by theorists of the Chomsky type. The argument
against the strong claim is the antifoundationalist argument: we can
never get to the side of our beliefs and, therefore, any perspective we
have on one or more of them will be grounded in others of them in
relation to which we can have no perspective because we have no distance.
The weak claim begins by accepting this argument but still manages to
find a space in which theory does its special work: although we can never
get an absolute perspective on our beliefs, we can still get a perspective
on *some* of our beliefs in relation to some others; and if this happens, it
may be that from within the enclosure of our beliefs we will spy contra-

dictions of which we had been unaware and, thereby, be provoked to
ask and answer some fundamental questions. In short, and in familiar
language, theory—or the foregrounding of assumptions—promotes
critical self-consciousness.

Now it is certainly the case that people are on occasion moved to
reconsider their assumptions and beliefs and then to change them, and
it is also the case that—as a consequence—there may be a corresponding
change in practice. The trouble is, such reconsiderations can be brought
about by almost anything and have no unique relationship to something
called "theory." Some years ago Lawrance Thompson published a biography
of Robert Frost in which the poet was revealed to have been a most
unpleasant, not to say evil, person. The book produced much consternation,
especially among those who had assumed that there was (or should be)
a correlation between the quality of a man's art and his character. Underlying this assumption was a traditional and powerful view of the
nature and function of literature. In that view (still held by many today),
literature is ennobling: it enlarges and refines the sensibility and operates
to make its readers better persons. It follows, then, that those who are
able to produce nobility in others should themselves be noble—but here
was an undeniably great artist who was, by all the evidence Thompson
had marshaled, perfectly vile. Presumably, Thompson's book induced
some who held this view to reconsider it; that is, they had been made
aware of their assumptions. What moved them, however, was not theory
but a work of traditional scholarship that did not even pretend to be
criticism.

The impulse to reexamine the principles underlying one's practice
can be provoked, moreover, by something that is not even within the
field of practice: by turning forty, or by a dramatic alteration in one's
economic situation, by a marriage, or by a divorce. Of course, it can also
be provoked by theory—but not necessarily. That is, you could engage
in the exercise of foregrounding your assumptions and even come to see
that some of them were incompatible with some piece of your practice
and, nevertheless, respond with a shrug, decide to let things be. The
man who declares himself committed to the redistribution of authority
and the diffusion of power may be an absolute autocrat in the classroom,
and when this is pointed out to him or when he points it out to himself,
he may mutter something about the limited attention span of today's
youth and go on as before. Even when theory produces self-consciousness,
it need not be "critical"; it need not be the prelude to change. Once again,
we reach the conclusion that there is no sense in which theory is special:
it can not provide us with a perspective independent of our beliefs, and
the perspective it can occasionally (but not necessarily) provide on some
of our beliefs relative to others can be provided by much that is not
theory.

If one has followed the argument thus far, it begins to be difficult
to understand why anyone has ever thought that theory should have

consequences. Yet, since many have thought so and will continue to think so even after I have done, it is time to inquire into the reasons for their conviction. One reason, and a very powerful one, is the institutional success of philosophy in persuading us that the answers to its questions are directly relevant to everything we do when we are not doing philosophy. As Richard Rorty has put it:

> Philosophers usually think of their discipline as one which discusses perennial, eternal problems—problems which arise as soon as one reflects. . . . Philosophy can be foundational in respect to the rest of culture because culture is the assemblage of claims to knowledge, and philosophy adjudicates such claims.[17]

The idea, then, is that whatever the surface configurations of our actions, *at bottom* we are being guided by principles of the kind that philosophy takes as its special province. Thus, it is to philosophy that we should look to get a perspective on those principles and on the actions we perform in everyday life.

The relevance of philosophy to every aspect of human culture has been assumed for so long that it now seems less an assertion or an argument than a piece of plain common sense. But it is, in fact, an argument, and one whose content is the debatable proposition that almost everything we do is a disguised and probably confused version of philosophy. That proposition will begin to seem less plausible if we remember that philosophy is not the name of a natural kind but of an academic discipline and, moreover, of a discipline whose traditions are so special as to constitute a prima facie denial of its territorial ambitions. Philosophy is that area of inquiry in which one asks questions about the nature of knowledge, truth, fact, meaning, mind, action, and so forth, and gives answers that fall within a predictable range of positions called realism, idealism, relativism, pragmatism, materialism, mentalism, Platonism, Aristotelianism, Kantianism, and so forth. Of course, other areas of inquiry are similarly well developed and articulated and come complete with their own array of positions, problems, solutions, and decorums. One of these is literary criticism, where the task is the description and evaluation of verbal artifacts and the categories of interrogation are historical (Is it Romantic or neoclassic?), generic (Is it masque or drama?), formal (Is it episodic or organic?), stylistic (Is it Senecan or Ciceronian?).

Now although the traditions of philosophy and literary criticism display certain points of intersection and occasionally refer to each other, they are for all intents and purposes distinct, so much so that it is perfectly possible for someone wholly ignorant of one to operate quite successfully in the other. It makes no sense then to think that one is radically dependent on the other, to think, for example, that since there is something called "the philosophy of action" and since literary criticism is an action, anyone who wants to know how to do literary criticism should consult the philosophy of action. A literary critic already knows what to do simply by virtue of his being embedded in a field of practice; it is hard to see why his performance would be improved or altered by bringing to bear the categories and urgencies of another field of practice. Of course, it is always possible to step back from a field and put to it the kinds of questions that belong properly (that is, by history and convention) to philosophy, to ask, for example, what literary critics must believe about the world, truth, meaning, fact, evidence, and so forth, in order to go about their work in a way that seems to them at once routine and natural. But the lessons learned from such an interrogation would be philosophical, not literary, and the fact that it was possible to learn them would not prove that those who do criticism are really doing philosophy any more than the fact that every activity is potentially the object of philosophical analysis means that every activity is at base philosophical and should be ruled by philosophy's norms.

The point is obvious and, one would have thought, inescapable: philosophy is one thing and literary criticism is another. But the point has been obscured by the fact that in the past twenty-five years philosophy has become something that literary critics also do or attempt to do. That is, they attempt to do theory, which is another name for philosophy; and if the argument for the consequences of theory seems strong when theory is a separate discipline, it seems even stronger when theory is a component of the field it purports to govern. But if theory (or philosophy) is now a practice in literary studies, it differs more from its fellow practices than they do from each other. A formalist and a critic of myth may be at odds, but they are in the same line of work and contesting for the same privilege, the privilege of saying what this poem or novel or play means. Theory, on the other hand, disdains particular acts of interpretation and aspires to provide an account of interpretation in general—and just as a philosophical analysis of an activity is not an instance of that activity but of philosophy, so an account of interpretation is not an interpretation but an account. They are different games, and they remain different even when they are played by the same person.

That is to say, as things stand now, a worker in the field may hold this or that theoretical position—think of himself as a foundationalist or an antifoundationalist—and *also* be a practicing critic—think of himself as a Wordsworthian or a Miltonist. *But,* when he is performing as a Wordsworthian or a Miltonist, he will be asking the questions and giving the answers that belong to that tradition of inquiry and his theoretical position will quite literally be beside the point. I may be convinced, as in fact I am, that my sense of what is going on in a literary work is a function of my history, education, professional training, ideological affiliation, and so on, but that conviction will be of no effect when I set out to determine who is the hero of *Paradise Lost;* for at that moment all of the categories, distinctions, imperatives, and urgencies that might at some other time become the object of a metacritical investigation will be firmly in place and form the enabling conditions of my actions. In short, theory is not consequential even when the practitioner is himself a theorist. Indeed, the practitioner may cease to be a theorist or may awake one morning (as I predict we all will) to find that theory has passed from the scene and still continue in his life's work without ever missing a beat.

This conclusion may seem to fly in the face of the evidence provided by those critics who, apparently, changed their practice when they changed their theory, who now discover aporias and radical de-centerings where they used to discover irony and unity. Doesn't this evidence itself constitute a strong empirical case for the consequences of theory?[18] Not at all— what it indicates is that thematizing remains the primary mode of literary criticism and that, as an action, thematizing can find its materials in theory as well as in anything else. In thematic criticism a work is discovered to be the literary expression or consideration of such and such concerns, be they economic or psychological, political or military, sexual, culinary, or whatever. What the thematic critic then produces are economic or psychological or sociological or political or philosophical readings. He does *not* produce—that is, he does not do—economics, psychology, sociology, political science, or philosophy. He may *quarry* these and other disciplines for vocabulary, distinctions, concerns, and so forth—indeed, it is hard to see what else he could do—but to quarry from a discipline is not to become a practitioner of it. If I propose a religious reading of George Herbert's lyrics, am I practicing religion? If I read Gustave Flaubert in the light of medical knowledge in the nineteenth century, am I practicing medicine? Obviously not—and neither, when I find that a work is "about" the limits of language, or the conditions of assertion, or the relativity of truth, am I doing theory. If I were practicing religion, I would be urging, chastising, and preaching; if I were practicing medicine, I would be setting bones and handing out prescriptions; and if I were practicing theory, I would either be arguing for a set of formal and explicit rules or arguing that rules of that kind are never available. I would not be analyzing the way in which such arguments are distributed over a range of characters in a novel or underlie the dramatic structure of the Romantic lyric. It is only because theory as a form of practice now shares an institutional or disciplinary home with literary criticism that its thematization is taken as evidence of its power to alter literary criticism. In fact, the power flows in the other direction: like any other discipline or body of materials that is made into thematic hay, theory is not so much the consequential agent of a change as it is the passive object of an appropriation.

We have now achieved what appears to be a dramatic reversal. At the outset, the strong thesis in the field was that theory has consequences and that they are far-reaching and fundamental, but now theory has been deprived of any consequentiality whatsoever and stands revealed as the helpless plaything of the practice it claimed to inform. But certainly we have gone too far, and it is time to admit what everyone knows: theory has consequences; not, however, because it stands apart from and can guide practice but because it is itself a form of practice and therefore is consequential for practice as a matter of definition.[19] That is, any account of what now makes up the practice of literary criticism must include theory, which means that there was a time when theory was not a part of criticism's practice, and the fact that it now is has made a difference, has been consequential.

Of course, as consequences go, this is pretty low-level, but there is more. As a practice, theory has all the political and institutional consequences of other practices. Those who do it can be published, promoted, fired, feted, celebrated, reviled; there can be symposia devoted to it, journals committed to it; there can be departments of theory, schools of theory; it can be a rallying cry ("Give me theory or give me death!"), a banner, a target, a program, an agenda. All of these (and more) are consequences, and they would not be possible if there were no theory. But although these are certainly the consequences of theory, they are not theoretical consequences; that is, they are not the consequences of a practice that stands in a relationship of precedence and mastery to other practices. There is a world of difference between saying that theory is a form of practice and saying that theory informs practice: to say the one is to claim for theory no more than can be claimed for anything else; to say the other is to claim everything. So, even though the thesis that theory has no consequences holds only when the consequences are of a certain kind, they are the only consequences that matter, since they are the consequences that would mark theory off as special.

We can test this by thinking about the consequences that would satisfy a theorist. Surely Chomsky's theory has had consequences: it has revolutionized a discipline and extended its sway; its terms and goals structure everything that happens in the field; but it has not had (and, by my argument, could not have) the consequences of its claims—it has not provided the formal and algorithmic model of language acquisition and use whose promise generated all the activity in the first place. The theory's success, in short, has been largely political; as such, it is a success that can hardly be comforting to Chomsky since the political is what he, like every other theorist, desires to rise above. Paradoxically, the triumph of Chomskian theory from an institutional point of view is an illustration of its failure from the point of view of its fondest hope, the hope to transcend point of view by producing a picture of the language that holds for any or all institutions and is beholden to none. Chomsky is in the position of every other theorist: the consequences he seeks are impossible, and the consequences to which he has clear right and title make him indistinguishable from any other political agent and render theory a category about which there is nothing particular—because there is nothing general—to say.

There is nothing either particular or general to say about theory's political consequences because, while they are palpable, they are not predictable; they do not follow *from* theory but are something that *befalls* theory—although, again, not necessarily and not always in the same way. As a practice, theory will cut a different figure in different disciplines; only in philosophy will changes in theory receive immediate and consequential attention. But that is because philosophy (at least in the analytic tradition) *is* theory, is the foundational project Rorty describes. Thus, to say that in philosophy a change in theory will change practice is only to say that when practice changes, it changes. In literary criticism, on the other hand, theory is only one practice among many, and its impact has varied with different locations and universities. In some places in the United States, the appearance of a theoretical manifesto in *New Literary History, Diacritics,* or *Critical Inquiry* will be Monday-morning news to which one must respond; in other places it will be heard, if it is heard at all, as the report of a minor skirmish on a foreign field of battle. In a discipline of such diversity with respect to theory, the question of its consequences cannot even be meaningfully put.

In the world of legal studies, the case is different again. There theory has recently become the center of debate, in large part because of a single issue, the legitimacy of judicial review, or, as it is sometimes called, the "countermajoritarian difficulty."[20] The difficulty takes the form of a question: How, in a democratic system, can one justify the fact that a group of men and women, who are appointed for life, pass judgment on the validity of legislation enacted by the elected representatives of the people? This question is quite literally a demand for theory, for a justifying argument that does not presuppose the interests of any party or the supremacy of any political goal or borrow its terms from the practice it would regulate. For the foundationalists, only such an argument will guarantee the coherence of the legal process—it simply *must* be found; the failure so far of the efforts to find it leads the antifoundationalists, on the other hand, to conclude that the legal process is political through and through and is therefore a sham. Both parties agree that the issue of judicial review is "the most fundamental in the extensive domain of constitutional law" and that the stakes are very high.[21] As long as that agreement continues, theory is likely to flourish as a consequential form of legal practice.

Here, then, are three disciplines, in each of which theory is differently consequential, and those differences themselves are not stable but contingent and changeable. Philosophy and theory have not always been one, and still are not in some parts of the world—and may not even be so in our part of the world if Rorty and some others have anything to say about it. Theory has not always been a glamour stock in literary studies and has already ceased to be a growth industry; if the urgency attached in the legal world to the issue of judicial review should ever fade, theory could fade with it (although if it has become well enough established, it might migrate to another issue). Will it fade? Will it rise in other disciplines hitherto innocent of it? Will the consequences of its appearance or demise be large or small? These and other questions could be answered only if there were a general account of theory's career, but since the determining factors will always be local and contingent—who could have predicted that the emigration of European scholars in the late 1930s would bring literary theory to the United States or that mar-ketplace conditions in the humanities would bring it (by way of disgruntled Ph.D.'s) to the law—no such account is available and we must wait upon the event. If the question of theory's consequences is itself not theoretical but empirical, it can only receive an empirical answer in the form of specific and historical investigations into the consequences that this or that theory did or did not have. The result of such investigations will vary—in some cases, there will be virtually nothing to report and, in others, the report will fill volumes—but in no case will the chronicling of theory's consequences demonstrate that theory has—by right, as an inherent property—consequences.

Will there be consequences to an argument against theory's conse-quences? Since that too is an empirical question, the answer is "Time will tell," but there are some consequences that would seem to be either likely or unlikely. A likely consequence attaches to the issue of justification. Should it happen that everyone were persuaded by the "no consequences" argument (an outcome that is itself extremely unlikely), the search for certain kinds of justification might very well cease or, at least, be carried on with altered hopes, and that would be a consequence. To return for a moment to the context of legal studies and the "countermajoritarian difficulty," the issue would lose its urgency and the debate would continue, if it continued, on different terms, if all parties were brought to see (1) that the demand for a justification of judicial review which did not pre-suppose but bracketed the interests, goals, agendas, lines of authority, and so on, already in place was a demand for something at once unob-tainable and empty, and (2) that the unavailability of such a justification proved not that everything was a sham but that justifications are always interested and acquire their intelligibility and force from the very prac-tices of which they are a public defense. That is, if both parties could be brought to see that political justifications are the only kind there is and that this fact does not render argument nugatory but necessary, they might fall to recommending their contrasting agendas for the frankly political consequences they would be likely to have and not for a theoretical purity they could never achieve. Such a turn of events would not change very much, since, if I am right, every argument is already interested and political no matter what its theoretical trappings—but at least certain kinds of objections would no longer have very much force and certain kinds of appeals would no longer seem tainted.

On the other side, there is at least one consequence of the success of the "no consequences" argument that is not only unlikely, but impossible, and can be ruled out in advance. The case for theory's inconsequentiality, even if it is persuasive, will not return us to some precritical state, whether it be thought of as a state of innocence or of know-nothing ignorance. The consequences of theory as a form of practice are real even if the consequences of theory as a foundational or antifoundational project could not possibly exist—indeed, theory's "practical" consequences are real *because* its "theoretical" consequences could not exist. The discrediting of theory could have the consequence of returning us to some uncontaminated or unredeemed practice only if theory were the independent and abstract calculus of its strongest claims. The fact that theory is not and could not be that calculus and therefore could not have the consequences of its claims assures that it will always have the political consequences I have been describing. Although theory cannot be a lever for change from the outside, its existence on the inside—within the field of practice—is evidence that a change has already occurred, a change in which its mode of interrogation has now joined or displaced others. That change cannot be reversed, and its effects will continue long after the formal program of theory has been abandoned.

Will it be abandoned? Will theory stop?—certainly not as a result of arguments against it, mine or anyone else's. Arguments against theory only keep it alive, by marking it as a site of general concern. Theory will stop only when it has played out its string, run its course, when the urgencies and fears of which it is the expression either fade or come to be expressed by something else. This is already happening in literary studies, and there could be no surer sign of it than the appearance in recent years of several major anthologies—by Josué Harari, Jane Tompkins, Robert Young—and of series that bear titles like New Accents but report only on what is old and well digested. The fading away of theory is signaled not by silence but by more and more talk, more journals, more symposia, and more entries in the contest for the right to sum up theory's story. There will come a time when it is a contest no one will want to win, when the announcement of still another survey of critical method is received not as a promise but as a threat, and when the calling of still another conference on the function of theory in our time will elicit only a groan. That time may have come: theory's day is dying; the hour is late; and the only thing left for a theorist to do is to say so, which is what I have been saying here, and, I think, not a moment too soon.

1. See my *Is There a Text in This Class?: The Authority of Interpretive Communities* (Cambridge, Mass., 1980), p. 370. For a response to the "no consequences" claim, see Mary Louise Pratt, "Interpretive Strategies/Strategic Interpretations: On Anglo-American Reader Response Criticism," *Boundary 2* 11 (Fall–Winter 1982–83): 222.

2. E. D. Hirsch, Jr., *The Aims of Interpretation* (Chicago, 1976), p. 18. I should note here that while I agree in general with Steven Knapp and Walter Benn Michaels on what is and is not a theoretical enterprise, I think them mistaken in their choice of particular

examples. Stylistics, narratology, and prosody are, it seems to me, paradigm instances of theory in the strong sense. As I have argued elsewhere (see *Is There a Text?*, chaps. 2 and 10), the entire project of stylistics is an effort to produce a taxonomy of observable formal features which can then be correlated in some mechanical or rule-governed way with a set of corresponding significances and/or effects. In short, if stylistics were ever to succeed (and I am certain that it will not), it would be an engine of interpretation, a method, a theory. One sure sign of a theoretical enterprise is the lengths its proponents will go to in order to pursue it. It seems to me extremely unlikely that stylisticians would have built their formidable apparatuses and worked out their complex formalizations only so as to be able to produce a new reading of James Joyce's "Eveline." The same goes for narratology and for prosody, at least in its transformational or Halle-Keyser version.

3. Hirsch, *Aims of Interpretation*, p. 18.

4. Cicero *De inventione* 2. 11. 37; and see Raoul Berger, *Government by Judiciary: The Transformation of the Fourteenth Amendment* (Cambridge, Mass., 1977).

5. See John Lyons, *Noam Chomsky*, rev. ed. (New York, 1978), p. 37.

6. Jerrold J. Katz and Thomas G. Bever, "The Fall and Rise of Empiricism," in Bever, Katz, and D. Terrence Langendoen, *An Integrated Theory of Linguistic Ability* (New York, 1976), p. 12; all further references to this work, abbreviated "FRE," will be included in the text.

7. Noam Chomsky, *Aspects of the Theory of Syntax* (Cambridge, Mass., 1965), p. 3; all further references to this work, abbreviated *ATS*, will be included in the text.

8. In the jargon of the trade these are called "performance factors" and belong to the study of utterances as opposed to sentences: "Sentences are abstract objects which are not tied to a particular context, speaker, or time of utterance. Utterances, on the other hand, are datable events, tied to a particular speaker, occasion and context" (Neil Smith and Deirdre Wilson, *Modern Linguistics: The Results of Chomsky's Revolution* [Bloomington, Ind., 1979], p. 45). Utterances are ranked on a scale of "acceptability" according to the conditions—cultural and, therefore, variable—of their production; sentences, on the other hand, are ranked on a scale of grammaticality or well-formedness according to the invariant rules of a formal system. On this point, see F. R. Palmer, *Semantics: A New Outline* (Cambridge, 1976), p. 8.

9. Judith Greene, *Psycholinguistics: Chomsky and Psychology* (Baltimore, 1972), p. 28.

10. That is, one must begin, as Smith and Wilson observe, by "separating linguistic from non-linguistic knowledge" (*Modern Linguistics*, p. 32), but it is precisely the possibility of that separation that is denied by the argument I am mounting here.

11. See my *Is There a Text?*, pp. 281–92.

12. That is why the history of Chomskian linguistics is a history of counterexamples to what are offered as *the* rules: since rules have been extrapolated from an assumed (if unacknowledged) context, the descriptions they assign will not seem perspicuous to someone who is operating from within *another* assumed (if unacknowledged) context. Of course any proposed alternative system of rules will be vulnerable to exactly the same challenge.

In a searching and rigorous critique of a draft of this paper, Joseph Graham of Tulane University objects that I misrepresent the Chomsky project in several respects. Echoing some of the arguments in Chomsky's *Rules and Representations* (Woodbridge Lectures, nos. 3, 11, 78 [New York, 1980]), Graham contends, among other things, that the notion of "theory" as it appears in my discussion of Chomsky is far too strong and does not correspond to any claims Chomsky actually makes; that I fail to distinguish between "universal grammar" as an innate biological constraint on the set of possible "core" grammars and one or more of those possible grammars; that I blur the crucial distinction, on which so much depends, between grammatical and pragmatic competence and, thereby, ask more of the grammar than it could ever deliver; and that no theoretical enterprise is "demonstrative" in the sense that I use the word, for all scientific inquiry proceeds on the basis of "abduction or inference to the best explanation." To this I would reply, first, that my account of the Chomsky project and its claims is derived from statements made by Chomsky and some of his more faithful followers and that even if, as Graham says, the theory has been modified and clarified in recent years, the euphoria with which it was received and promoted in its early stages shows that it was for many the basis of what I call foundationalist "theory hope." Moreover, some of the differences between Graham and me stem from the different and opposing traditions in which we stand—he in the tradition of cognitive psychology with its interest in innate properties and inaccessible mental operations, and I in the practice and convention-centered tradition that includes Ludwig Wittgenstein, W. V. Quine, Hilary Putnam, Richard Rorty, and Donald Davidson, in addition to Jacques Derrida, Michel Foucault, and other continental thinkers. Presumably, for example, Graham would hear with equanimity and even with approval Chomsky's suggestion that knowledge and certainty may have little or nothing to do with grounding, justification, reasons, habits, skill, induction, and learning, and everything to do with genetic mechanisms that have yet to be specified, while to my ears the same suggestion sounds counterintuitive and even uninteresting (see Chomsky, *Rules and Representations*, pp. 92–109, 134–36, and 234). To be sure, there is more to be said about these matters, and Graham promises to say them in a series of forthcoming essays, but for the time being I will stick with my present formulations.

13. Rorty, *Consequences of Pragmatism (Essays: 1972–1980)* (Minneapolis, 1982), p. 162.

14. Keith Lehrer, *Knowledge* (Oxford, 1974), p. 17.

15. Israel Scheffler, *Science and Subjectivity* (Indianapolis, 1967), p. 19. For similar statements, see Hirsch, *Aims of Interpretation*, pp. 152–55, and Owen M. Fiss, "Objectivity and Interpretation," *Stanford Law Review* 34 (Apr. 1982): 763.

16. Thomas Grey, "Supplementing the Constitution"; unpublished paper, quoted with permission of the author.

17. Rorty, *Philosophy and the Mirror of Nature* (Princeton, N.J., 1979), p. 3.

18. This is the argument made by Steven Mailloux in "Truth or Consequences: On Being Against Theory."

19. See Mailloux, pp. 70–71. Mailloux also asserts that theory is a form of practice, but we differ in our conclusions. He concludes that "theory does change practice" and cites as two examples the "theoretical assumptions" that "guide" Edward Said's "practical analyses of Orientalism" and the "New Critical proscriptions against the intentional and affective fallacies" which led critics to avoid "extrinsic approaches" and focus instead on "intrinsic elements in the literary text itself" (Mailloux, pp. 70, 69, 70). To take the second example first, the Wimsatt-Beardsley injunction against taking into account the intentions of the author or the responses of the reader is exactly parallel to the injunction in the legal institution against looking beyond the Constitution itself to supplemental contexts: both make the same impossible recommendations and give the same unfollowable advice. That is, one may *say* "Consider only the text and not its extrinsic circumstances or the accident of its variable effects," but in fact any text one considers will have come into view only against the contextual—including intentional and affective—circumstances that are supposedly being excluded or bracketed. In short, someone may well think that he is adhering to Wimsatt and Beardsley's theoretical strictures, but the truth is that he could not possibly do so. What he can do is present his argument in terms that make no mention of intention or affect; although that will certainly be a consequence of the pressure exerted by Wimsatt and Beardsley's pronouncements, it will not be a consequence of their theory in the sense of being answerable to its claims and hopes. One cannot, as I have said above, attribute consequences of a theoretical kind to a program that cannot be executed.

The example of Said and *Orientalism* can be assimilated to the discussion of the two legislators who are committed respectively to libertarian and utilitarian principles. It is certainly the case, as Mailloux asserts, that Said's assumptions guide his practice, but assumptions aren't theories, that is, they are not systematic procedures for generating valid conclusions—they are the *assertion* of conclusions which, when put to work as an interpretive "window," will generate or validate themselves. Said's assumption—or conviction, or belief— is that Western discourse, including diplomatic and academic as well as fictional texts, has projected an image of the Orient that has, for all intents and purposes, become its reality.

Armed with this assumption, indeed operating as an extension of it, Said proceeds to redescribe texts as instances of a colonialism that does not know itself and is therefore even more powerful and insidious in its effects. But in producing these redescriptions, Said is not consulting a theory but extending a belief: when he urges his redescriptions on others, he is saying "Try on this belief; make it, rather than some other assumption, the content of your perception, and see what you see." It is a recommendation no more theoretical than a recommendation to think of the prefaces to Renaissance plays as part of the texts they introduce; either recommendation, if it is persuasive, will certainly alter practice but only because it will be a *practical* (not theoretical) recommendation, a recommendation to look at it this way rather than that way. To return to a formula used above, the Said example is an instance of something that has consequences but isn't a theory, and the Wimsatt-Beardsley example is an instance of something that is a theory and has consequences but not theoretical ones.

20. For a review and a discussion, see James A. Thomson, "An Endless but Productive Dialogue: Some Reflections on Efforts to Legitimize Judicial Review," *Texas Law Review* 61 (Dec. 1982): 743–64.

21. Ibid., p. 745.

Philosophy without Principles

Richard Rorty

My colleague E. D. Hirsch has skillfully developed the consequences for literary interpretation of a "realistic" epistemological position which he formulates as follows: "If we could not distinguish a content of consciousness from its contexts, we could not know any object at all in the world." Given that premise, it is easy for Hirsch to infer that "without the stable determinacy of meaning there can be no knowledge in interpretation."[1] A lot of people disagree with Hirsch on the latter point, and they look to philosophy for replies to the premise from which it was inferred. But it is not clear where in philosophy they should look: To epistemology? Ethics?[2] Philosophy of language? What Jacques Derrida calls "a new logic, . . . a graphematics of iterability"?[3] Where do we find first principles from which to deduce an anti-Hirsch argument?

I want to argue that there is no clear or straight answer to this question and that there need be none. I shall begin by criticizing the strategy used against Hirsch and others by my fellow pragmatists Steven Knapp and Walter Benn Michaels. They think that one can start with philosophy of language and straighten things out by adopting a correct account of meaning. I share their desire to refute Hirsch, their admiration for Stanley Fish, and their view that "theory"—when defined as "an attempt to govern interpretations of particular texts by appealing to an account of interpretation in general"—has got to go (p. 11, and see p. 30). But they want to defend this position by exposing a mistake which they think common to all theory so defined: an error about the relation between meaning and intention. They assert that "what is intended and

Reprinted from the March 1985 issue of *Critical Inquiry*.

what is meant are identical" and that one will look for an "account of interpretation in general" only if one fails to recognize this identity (pp. 17, 11). Such failure leads to an attempt to connect meaning and intention (as in Hirsch) or to disconnect them (as in Paul de Man). But such attempts must fail, for they presuppose a break "between language and speech acts" which does not exist (p. 21).

Knapp and Michaels defend this latter claim by saying that marks which are shaped like a sentence of English do not count as language unless the marks are backed up by an intention—unless they are inscribed by somebody who meant something by them. If one grants this point, Knapp and Michaels argue, one will not, with speech-act theorists such as H. P. Grice, distinguish between what sentences mean and what a given utterer means by them on a given occasion. Grice would say of a pattern of marks created on a beach by random wave motion that it means whatever the sentence it has been construed to token means, even though nobody ever meant anything by it. Knapp and Michaels would deny this (see p. 21, esp. n.13).[4] For Grice's distinction opens up the logical space they want to close: the space in which one asks the traditional interpretive question "Granted that the sentence means such and such, did its author use it to mean that on this particular occasion?"

Since I regard this as a useful question, I should like to keep the space open and, thus, to side with Grice. So I would urge that anything—a wave pattern, an arrangement of stars, the spots on a rock—can be treated not only as language but as any given sentence of English if one can find some way to map its features onto the semantic and syntactic features of that sentence (and other actual and possible patterns or arrangements or spots on the other sentences of English). "Linguisticality" is, on this view, cheap. You can impute it to anything simply by working out a translation scheme, just as you can impute goodness to anything by imagining a desirable end to which it can be a means. The question of whether the thing is really a sentence or whether we are simply pretending it is, is just as bad as the question of whether goodness is objective or subjective. Both questions should be eschewed by us pragmatists, since both presuppose Hirsch's Husserlian distinction between content and context, between essential and accidental properties (as opposed to the harmless distinction between normal or familiar properties and abnormal or unfamiliar ones). So I think Knapp and Michaels should not go out on a metaphysical limb by saying that the absence of an

Richard Rorty is Kenan Professor of Humanities at the University of Virginia. He is the author of *Consequences of Pragmatism (Essays: 1972-1980),* among other works, and is currently writing a book on Martin Heidegger.

intending inscriber means that the marks in the sands are not words. For this leaves them open wider than necessary to Adena Rosmarin's question "Now how do Knapp and Michaels know *this?*" and to her charge that "their premises beg their question" (Rosmarin, p. 86).

Continuing this more-pragmatic-than-thou line, I would urge that Knapp and Michaels not try to undergird Fish by constructing a philosophy of language which will make it illicit to form a general theory of interpretation. Rather, we should follow W. V. Quine, Donald Davidson, and Jeffrey Stout in saying that the question "What is the meaning of a text?" is as useless as the question "What is the nature of the good?"[5] Pragmatists are supposed to treat everything as a matter of a choice of context and nothing as a matter of intrinsic properties. They dissolve objects into functions, essences into momentary foci of attention, and knowing into success at reweaving a web of beliefs and desires into more supple and elegant folds. So I think that Knapp and Michaels' distrust of "theory's epistemological project" (defined by them as "bas[ing] interpretation on a direct encounter with its object, an encounter undistorted by the influence of the interpreter's particular beliefs") would be better expressed by a direct attack on the image of "direct encounter with objects" than by an attack on Grice's handy distinction between more and less familiar contexts in which to place words (p. 25). Knapp and Michaels' claim that meaning is identical with intention suggests that we put the text in whatever context we find useful and then call the result a discovery of the author's intention.[6] But why call it anything in particular? Why not just put in a context, describe the advantages of having done so, and forget the question of whether one has got at either its "meaning" or "the author's intention"?

But Rosmarin's metaphilosophical question arises at the next level up. How do I, how does any pragmatist, know that there are no direct encounters with objects? Don't my premises beg all the interesting questions? They do indeed. There is a large circle of concepts—for example, knowledge, truth, object, science, reference, meaning, intentionality, and so on—such that a realist or a pragmatist analysis of any one will supply premises from which to deduce a parallel analysis of any of the others. There is no natural order of priority among such concepts which tells you how to start at the very top and work your way down. Nor is there any such order among the various areas of philosophy. You can start with metaphysics and move down to epistemology, or with semantics and work down to metaphysics, or with epistemology and work down to ethics and down from there to metaphysics. It may seem, consequently, that all of us who debate these matters start out with either Hirsch-like or Fish-like intuitions and then go round in circles, defending them in one guise by appealing to them in another.

If one thinks of philosophy as entirely a matter of deductive argument, then this game of mirrors will, indeed, be one's only recourse. But one can also think of philosophy in other ways—in particular, as a matter of telling stories: stories about why we talk as we do and how we might avoid continuing to talk that way. When you find yourself at an argumentative impasse, baffled by your opponent's refusal to stop asking questions which you think you really should not have to answer, you can always shift the ground by raising questions about the vocabulary he or she is using. You can point out that the issue is biased in one's opponent's favor by the unfortunate jargon which has developed, a jargon which gives one's opponent an unfair advantage. You can use historical narratives to show why the issue previously discussed is moot and why it needs to be reformulated in terms which are, alas, not yet available.

This strategy of using narrative where argument fails is what makes Heideggerian and Derridean attempts to "problematize" the vocabulary used by contemporary philosophers so attractive. Inconclusive debates between reformers of the Right and the Left make revolutionaries look good. So it is tempting to think that the pragmatist should stop offering analyses of knowledge and truth and instead fall back on a quasi-Heideggerian account of how we got into our present dead end. Derrida tells us that unless we go back and deconstruct what Plato built, we shall always be haunted by his ghost—by the idea that there is some natural starting point and resting-place for thought, something like Hirsch's context-free contents of consciousness. Accordingly, one might think that only by overcoming the metaphysics of presence—ceasing to use not only "meaning" and "intention" but all the bad old Platonic oppositions which make these notions seem inevitable—could pragmatists like Knapp and Michaels end "theory."

Pragmatists and Derrideans are, indeed, natural allies. Their strategies supplement each other admirably. But there is no natural priority of one strategy over the other. It is not the case that we shall have rational grounds for rejecting realism only if we can overcome the metaphysics of presence. The notion of "rational grounds" is not in place once one adopts a narrative strategy. (That is why Derrida looks bad whenever he attempts argument on his opponents' turf; those are the passages in which he becomes a patsy for John Searle.) For if we ever did get rid of all the jargon of the tradition, we should not even be able to state the realist's position, much less argue against it. The enemy would have been forgotten rather than refuted. If Derrida ever got his "new logic," he would not be able to use it to outargue his opponents. Whatever a "graphematics of iterability" might be good for, it would be of no use in polemic. The metaphysics of presence was designed precisely to facilitate argument, to make questions like "How do you know?" seem natural, and to make a search for first principles and natural resting-places seem obligatory. It assumes that all of us can tell such a resting-place when we see it and that at least some of our thoughts are already there. You can't argue against that assumption by using the vocabulary of the tradition, but neither can you *argue* that the tradition is wrong in its choice of vocabulary. You can argue only against a proposition, not against a vocabulary. Vocabularies get discarded after looking bad in comparison with other vocabularies, not as a result of an appeal to overarching metavocabularies in which criteria for vocabulary choice can be formulated.

This means that narrative philosophy should not be expected to fill gaps left vacant by argumentative philosophy. Rather, the importance of narrative philosophy is that persuasion is as frequently a matter of getting people to drop a vocabulary (and the questions they phrase within it) as of deductive argument. So, though I think Rosmarin is right in suggesting that the linguistic reform which Knapp and Michaels propose is the wrong way (because it is a needlessly paradoxical way) to make their antitheoretical point, I do not mean that linguistic reform is a generally bad—or ineffective—strategy, nor that Rosmarin's question "How do you know?" should be pressed. What is wrong with this question is that, as asked by Socrates and the Platonic tradition, it assumes that we know what knowledge is like and can tell when we have got it. But this notion of knowledge as an introspectable state is just one more Platonic myth. The right way to construe this question is "Why do you find what you just said persuasive?" That is a question which ignores the traditional distinctions between reasons and causes, psychology and logic, rhetoric and demonstration. It is a *practical* question, a polite version of the question "What am I going to have to do to convince you?"

To return to the question of theory, one can be against what Knapp and Michaels define as the attempt to get outside practice and regulate it, and agree nonetheless with another of their critics, Steven Mailloux, that theory should "continue doing what all discursive practices do: attempt to persuade its readers to adopt its point of view, its way of seeing texts and the world" (Mailloux, p. 71).[7] For, in its unobjectionable sense, "theory" just means "philosophy." One can still have philosophy even after one stops arguing deductively and ceases to ask where the first principles are coming from, ceases to think of there being a special corner of the world—or the library—where they are found. In particular, I take "literary theory," as the term is currently used in America, to be a species of philosophy, an attempt to weave together some texts traditionally labeled "philosophical" with other texts not so labeled. It names the practice of splicing together your favorite critics, novelists, poets, and such, and your favorite philosophers. This is not exactly what Mailloux calls "metapractice (practice about practice)," for that term suggests a vertical relationship, in which some practices are at higher levels than others (Mailloux, p. 71). Rather, it is just more practice of the same sort, using a slightly different set of raw materials. Thinking of it this way helps one get rid of the idea that philosophy is somehow on another level. It lets one think of "philosophical" and "literary" texts as grist for the same mill.

To conclude on a blatantly practical note, I would offer as one reason in favor of my version of pragmatism and against Knapp and Michaels' that they are driven•to the conclusion that we should "eliminate the 'career option' of writing and teaching theory" (p. 105). In my view, this career option consists in an opportunity to discuss philosophy books — as well as novels, poems, critical essays, and so forth—with literature students. Knapp and Michaels, however, construe it as the attempt to supply foundations for literary interpretation. I would hope that the latter rhetoric could be discarded while the career option remains. The recent emergence of this option seems to me one of the healthier features of American academic life. For, as Paul Alpers has remarked, courses in "literary theory" have become "ports of entry" for a tradition of European philosophical thought which had been neglected in America. There is no particular reason why this tradition should be taught in literature departments rather than in philosophy departments, but there is also no particular reason why it should not be. It should certainly be taught somewhere in our universities, and it seems to me greatly to the credit of our literature departments that they have given it a home.

1. E. D. Hirsch, Jr., *The Aims of Interpretation* (Chicago, 1976), pp. 3, 1.

2. See ibid., where Hirsch offers a "fundamental ethical maxim for interpretation" which, he says, "claims no privileged sanction from metaphysics or analysis" (p. 90). Here and elsewhere Hirsch suggests that it may be ethics rather than epistemology which provides the principles that govern interpretation. There remain other passages, however, in which he retains the view, conspicuous in his earlier writings, that an analysis of the idea of knowledge is the ultimate justification for his approach.

3. Jacques Derrida, "Limited Inc abc . . . ," *Glyph* 2 (1977): 219.

4. It seems to me that Knapp and Michaels are wrong in thinking of John Searle and H. P. Grice as "arriv[ing] at determinate meanings by adding intentions [to language]" (p. 21). They are, rather, distinguishing between two sets of intentions—the ones normally had by users of a sentence and some special ones had, or possibly had, by an individual user. More generally, I cannot think of anybody who would deny that one has language only where there is a system of community intentions, of conventions (in the sense analyzed by David Lewis). So I am not sure that there are any "anti-intentionalist accounts of meaning" (a phrase used by Knapp and Michaels; see p. 15). Paul de Man (cited as an example of an anti-intentionalist; see Knapp and Michaels, "A Reply to Our Critics," p. 100 n.4) does not seem to me to hold such a view. Nor, I think, does Michel Foucault. I would take Foucault to be saying that one can tell useful historical stories if one takes language rather than human beings as one's subject, bracketing questions about why human beings changed their linguistic habits. But that does not commit him to the claim that language can exist without human beings establishing conventions, any more than atheistic idealism is committed to the view that minds existed before rocks did. Questions about what comes first in causal sequence are irrelevant in both cases.

5. See Jeffrey Stout, "What Is the Meaning of a Text?," *New Literary History* 14 (Autumn 1982): 1–12.

6. See Knapp and Michaels: "Any interpreter of any utterance or text, within the institution of professional literary criticism or not, is, if we are right, attempting to understand the author's intention" (p. 105). It seems to me that Knapp and Michaels do not satisfactorily answer Hirsch's claim that their arguments show only that "a text's meaning . . . must always be what *an* author intends it to mean" and not that it "must always be what *its* author intends it to mean" (Hirsch, p. 50).

7. Cf.: "What Knapp and Michaels treat as inherent and erroneous dissociations might be more subtly and profitably discussed as analytic strategies" (Rosmarin, p. 85). In their "Reply," Knapp and Michaels say that Mailloux and Rosmarin are both "negative theorists" (p. 100). (As Knapp and Michaels define it, negative theory tries to preserve "the purity of language from the distortion of speech acts" [p. 21].) But I should think that the "hostility to method" which Knapp and Michaels say characterizes negative theory was independent of any such motive (p. 21; and see n.4 above).

A Reply to Richard Rorty: What Is Pragmatism?

Steven Knapp and Walter Benn Michaels

We are grateful to Stanley Fish for demonstrating what "Against Theory" had merely assumed, that the only kind of theory worth attacking is the kind which claims to be more than just another form of practice. Some readers have thought that our arguments were directed against all general reflection about literature or criticism. Others have thought that we were resisting the encroachment on literary study of themes derived from politics, or psychoanalysis, or philosophy. These are plausible misreadings of our intention, since the term "theory" is indeed sometimes applied to any critical argument marked by historical or aesthetic generalization or by the reading of literature in terms of themes derived from other disciplines. But, as Fish shows, neither empirical generality nor thematic novelty is enough to make an argument theoretical in more than a trivial sense, that is, in a sense that marks it as importantly different in kind from other critical arguments. Theory in a nontrivial sense always consists in the attempt "to stand outside practice in order to govern practice from without," and this strong ("foundationalist") kind of theory is the kind whose coherence we deny (p. 30). It is also the kind of theory engaged in by the vast majority of those who consider themselves theorists— including many who might prefer to think of themselves as practicing theory in some weaker sense.

At the conclusion of "Philosophy without Principles," Richard Rorty appears to join those who think we are attacking theory in its weaker senses as well as in the strong sense just described. He suggests that eliminating the writing and teaching of theory would deprive literary

Reprinted from the March 1985 issue of *Critical Inquiry*.

scholars of "an opportunity to discuss philosophy books—as well as novels, poems, critical essays, and so forth—with literature students" (Rorty, p. 137). If this were the only issue between Rorty's version of pragmatism and ours, our disagreement would come to an immediate end, since nothing could be further from the aims of "Against Theory" than rendering a judgment about what books should be discussed in literary classrooms. But our disagreement runs deeper than debates about the curriculum. It involves, first, a fundamental disagreement about language and, second, an equally fundamental disagreement about the nature and consequences of pragmatism.

In a note to his discussion of our account of language and intention, Rorty writes, "It seems to me that Knapp and Michaels do not satisfactorily answer Hirsch's claim that their arguments show only that 'a text's meaning . . . must always be what *an* author intends it to mean' and not that it 'must always be what *its* author intends it to mean' " (Rorty, p. 137 n.6). This objection makes sense, it seems to us, only if one thinks that the distinction between what "*an*" author intends a text to mean and what "*its*" author intended it to mean is a distinction between two different interpretations of the same text—not two different interpretations of two *different* texts but two different interpretations of the *same* text, in other words, two competing interpretations. There's nothing controversial about different texts having different meanings. Controversy arises only when interpreters ascribe different meanings to what they regard as the same text. In our view, in fact, controversy arises only when there is a disagreement about what some particular author meant on some particular occasion, the occasion on which that author produced the text in question. There is never any point in choosing between what *its* author meant and what *an* author might have meant, since interpretive disagreements are never anything else but disagreements about what *its*, the text's, author meant. But Hirsch and Rorty maintain that a distinction between what *an* author means and what *its* author meant is relevant to disagreement about the meaning of a particular text. So they must think that a text remains the same text despite differences in author and occasion. What,

Steven Knapp is an assistant professor of English at the University of California, Berkeley; his book *Personification and the Sublime: Milton to Coleridge* is forthcoming. **Walter Benn Michaels,** an associate professor of English at the University of California, Berkeley, is working on the relation between literary and economic forms of representation in nineteenth-century America.

then, if not the fact of having been produced by a particular author on a particular occasion, do they think confers identity on a text?

One answer might be the formalist one: the identity of a text consists in the identity of a collection of marks. And, of course, a collection of marks does have an identity as a collection of marks, irrespective of its relation to any author. Marks produced by erosion, as in our wave-poem example, might be identical to marks produced by someone writing with a stick. But identity of marks becomes identity of text—marks become text—only when, as we argued in "Against Theory," the marks express an authorial intention. The formalist thinks that a collection of marks is in itself already a text and therefore already has some meaning whether or not it expresses anyone's intention. Neither Hirsch nor Rorty, however, thinks there can be intentionless meanings. Indeed, according to Rorty, *no one* thinks there can be intentionless meanings:

> It seems to me that Knapp and Michaels are wrong in thinking of John Searle and H. P. Grice as "arriv[ing] at determinate meanings by adding intentions [to language]". . . . They are, rather, distinguishing between two sets of intentions—the ones normally had by users of a sentence and some special ones had, or possibly had, by an individual user. More generally, I cannot think of anybody who would deny that one has language only where there is a system of community intentions, of conventions (in the sense analyzed by David Lewis). So I am not sure that there are any "anti-intentionalist accounts of meaning." [Rorty, p. 137 n.4]

If what gives a text its identity as a text is neither, as we think, its relation to a particular author and occasion nor, as formalists (if there are any) think, its meaning as a collection of marks, then what does? The choice between our position and the formalist position is a choice between reading a text as the expression of *its* author's intention and reading a text as the expression of *no* author's intention. But for both Rorty and Hirsch there is, as we have seen, a third possibility: reading a text as the expression of *an* author's intention. (They disagree, of course, about the desirability of this option.) But why does Rorty think that Hirsch's notion of *an* author's intention provides a relevant alternative to our account? According to Rorty, there is a "useful" "logical space" between "what sentences mean and what a given utterer means by them on a given occasion" (Rorty, p. 133). This is what Rorty glosses, in the note quoted above, as the distinction "between two sets of intentions—the ones normally had by users of a sentence and some special ones had, or possibly had, by an individual user." Rorty's notion of a sentence's normal intention corresponds to Hirsch's claim that one can read a text in terms of *an* author's meaning, while Rorty's notion of an individual user's special intention corresponds to Hirsch's claim that one can read a text in terms of *its* author's meaning. But what makes some intentions normal and others special? Rorty seems to be thinking of the distinction between special and normal intentions as if it were a distinction between *particular* intentions and some other kind.

In our view, however, normal intentions are just frequent particular ones. The "space" between these two sets of intentions is not logical but empirical. A text means what its author intended it to mean whether or not other authors on other occasions use the same marks (or noises) to say the same thing. What people normally mean when they shout "Fire!" might well be that something is burning. On some special occasion, however, someone might shout "Fire!" and mean by it "Discharge your weapon." In the first case, the speaker has an intention frequently had by other speakers on similar occasions; in the second case, not. Indeed, there could be a third case in which a speaker might shout "Fire!" and mean by it something that no one had ever meant before or would ever mean again. But in all three cases the relation between meaning and intention would be the same: the sentence would mean only what *its* speaker intended. The fact that, in the first case, the speaker meant what speakers usually mean by "Fire!" and, in the other cases, what speakers rarely or never mean by "Fire!" does not amount to a distinction between different kinds of meaning (sentence meaning and utterer's meaning, what *an* author intends and what *its* author intended) but only to a distinction between different meanings. Disagreement about the meaning of a text depends not on the possibility of different kinds of intention— on the logical choice between what *its* author intended and what *an* author intends—but only on the empirical difficulty of deciding what *its* author intended.

The distinction between two different kinds of authorial intention thus collapses. The only alternative to the intentionalism of "Against Theory" is a formalism that imagines the possibility not of two different kinds of intended meaning but of meaning that is not intended at all. Such a formalism is, of course, anathema to Hirsch, although, as we argued in "Against Theory," it is the position he is forced to hold. And, insofar as Rorty is seriously committed to keeping open a logical space between language and speech acts (sentence meaning and utterer's meaning), he too is forced to become the formalist whose existence he denies. He must believe that marks and noises can be language "even though nobody ever meant anything" by them. If, on the other hand, Rorty thinks that this distinction reduces to a logically uninteresting (and theoretically useless) difference between frequent and infrequent intentions, then his account of language is identical to ours. He must agree with our claim that, as he puts it, "marks which are shaped like a sentence of English do not count as language unless . . . inscribed by somebody who meant something by them" (Rorty, p. 133).

For Rorty, however, the real issue is not whether we are right or wrong about what makes something language. In fact, for him, the whole point of pragmatism is to render such questions fundamentally irrelevant. There's no point in asking what makes something language, since *anything* can be treated as language: "Anything—a wave pattern, an arrangement of stars, the spots on a rock—can be treated not only as language but as any given sentence of English. . . . 'Linguisticality' is, on this view, cheap." Hence, pragmatists "should not go out on a metaphysical limb" by trying to distinguish between what is language and what isn't: "The question of whether the thing is really a sentence or whether we are simply pretending it is, is just as bad as the question of whether goodness is objective or subjective. Both questions should be eschewed by us pragmatists" (Rorty, p. 133).

On one point, we agree: "linguisticality" is cheap. Anything can indeed be treated as an English sentence, as Rorty says, "if one can find some way to map its features onto the semantic and syntactic features of that sentence" (Rorty, p. 133). Anything that looks like English can be treated as language; anything that looks like any language can be treated as language; indeed, something that looks like no existing language can, if it is regarded as the expression of a linguistic intention, be treated as language.[1] Thus Rorty is right to say that anything can be treated as a sentence "whether the thing is really a sentence or whether we are simply pretending it is." We can think that any collection of marks is really being used to express an intention, or we can just pretend it is. But it doesn't follow from this that it makes no difference whether something is really language or not. If you really think that a noise you hear is someone shouting "Fire!" you might call the fire department. But if you are just pretending that the noise is language, you might not want to risk arrest for turning in a false alarm. If to ask whether a noise is really language is to "go out on a metaphysical limb," it is also to ask the kind of *"practical* question" that interpreters ask all the time (Rorty, pp. 133, 136). A position from which such questions would be "bad" could only be a position outside practice itself.

The attempt to occupy a position outside practice is theory. It is also, as we argued in "Against Theory," the attempt to occupy a position outside belief. What Rorty calls going "out on a metaphysical limb," we call having beliefs; his alternative to metaphysics (having beliefs) is theory (not having beliefs). But even *pretending* to believe something depends on believing something else. Pretending to believe that you hear someone shout "Fire!" depends on believing that you really don't. The difference between believing something and pretending (believing something else) is simultaneously a difference in practice and belief. The only point of pragmatism is the inseparability of practice and belief: as Charles Sanders Peirce wrote in "How to Make Our Ideas Clear," "Belief is a rule for action," and "different beliefs are distinguished by the different modes of action to which they give rise."[2]

From a pragmatist perspective, then, disagreements about language—or anything else—are always practical. (Even the disagreement between pragmatism and theory has one practical consequence: theorists write theory and pragmatists write against theory.) From Rorty's perspective, the practical nature of disagreement sooner or later makes argument pointless, a "game of mirrors," since "all of us who debate these matters" start out with "premises" or "intuitions" that "beg all the interesting questions" and then "go round in circles, defending them in one guise by appealing to them in another." For Rorty, the way out of this "argumentative impasse" is to replace argument with what he calls the "strategy of using narrative" (Rorty, pp. 134, 135). Since "persuasion is as frequently a matter of getting people to drop a vocabulary . . . as of deductive argument," we must learn to "think of philosophy in other ways—in particular, as a matter of telling stories: stories about why we talk as we do and how we might avoid continuing to talk that way" (Rorty, pp. 136, 134–35).

If the difference between argument and narrative is simply the difference between two strategies for getting people to change their views on some particular question (for example, on whether "Fire!" is language or just noise), then it reduces to nothing more than the difference between two styles of argument. Philosophers might be more easily convinced by narrative; literary critics, by deductive argument. There's no reason in principle why a pragmatist should prefer arguments to narratives or narratives to arguments. The essence of Rorty's pragmatism, however, lies in his sense that narrative ("telling stories" or what, in *Philosophy and the Mirror of Nature,* he calls "conversation") liberates us from a dependence on argument. It provides an alternative vision of philosophical discourse, one that will see "philosophers as conversational partners" instead of "seeing them as holding views on subjects of common concern" and that will "prevent conversation from degenerating into inquiry, into an exchange of views."[3] It provides this alternative because it is immune to the various forms of what he calls Adena Rosmarin's "metaphilosophical question": "How do Knapp and Michaels know" that "language and intention are inseparable"?; How does Richard Rorty "know that there are no direct encounters with objects"?; How does anyone know anything? (Rosmarin, p. 86; Rorty, p. 134). Narrative, or conversation, or what he calls "edifying philosophy" is immune to this question precisely because it makes no claim to know.[4]

How can there be a mode of discourse that makes no claim to know? Since, as we have argued in "Against Theory," a belief is nothing other than a claim to know something, the attempt to imagine a discourse that makes no claim to know must be an attempt to imagine a discourse independent of belief. But there is no discourse independent of belief.

Even telling stories about language (myths about its origins, legends about its growth, prophecies of its end) involves having beliefs about what language is, what it's for, and what it can do. Even if it were true, as Rorty suggests, that all such beliefs could be reduced to nothing more than unjustifiable intuitions, they could not for this reason be discarded. They could not be discarded because they would remain embedded in every form of practice, including every strategy designed to avoid them. The attempt to discard them is Rorty's attempt to escape practice and, by preserving the theoretical project that pragmatism exists only to oppose, to escape pragmatism.[5]

Our point is not really to accuse Rorty of being less pragmatist than we are. Our point is that no one, in practice, can ever be more or less pragmatist than we are. Our arguments from the start have taken the form of showing that whatever positions people think they hold on language, interpretation, and belief, in practice they are all pragmatists. They all think language is intentional, and they all think their beliefs are true. In theory, they may distinguish between speech acts and language, between having beliefs and claiming to know, between having true beliefs and really knowing. To think the distinction between these things matters or even to think that it doesn't matter—just to think there is a distinction— is to be a theorist. In practice, there are no such distinctions and, in practice, there are no theorists.

1. This lines up with our earlier remark that someone can use a noise to say something even if no one has ever before used it to say the same thing. Our further point here is that noises or marks can function as language even if no one has ever before used them to say *anything*. Together these remarks amount to the assertion that the prior existence of linguistic conventions is irrelevant to the question of whether something is language. Hence it is not necessarily true that, as Richard Rorty asserts in a note already cited, "one has language only where there is a system of community intentions, of conventions (in the sense analyzed by David Lewis)" (Rorty, p. 137 n.4). (The notion that conventions as analyzed by Lewis are essential to language has recently been criticized by Donald Davidson; see *Inquiries into Truth and Interpretation* [Oxford, 1984], pp. 276–78.) Our insistence in "Against Theory" that language is always intentional is no more than the positive side of the denial that preexisting forms, rules, or conventions are essential conditions of language.

2. Charles Sanders Peirce, "How to Make Our Ideas Clear," *Collected Papers of Charles Sanders Peirce*, ed. A. W. Burks, Charles Hartshorne, and Paul Weiss, 8 vols. (Cambridge, Mass., 1931–58), 5:255.

3. Rorty, *Philosophy and the Mirror of Nature* (Princeton, N.J., 1979), p. 372.

4. Ibid. On this point Rorty's position is strikingly similar to that of E. D. Hirsch, Jr., despite the fact that each defines his views in opposition to the other's. Pragmatism, according to Rorty, makes no claim even to know whether it is itself true. Instead, the "question of whether the pragmatist view of truth—that it is not a profitable topic—is itself *true* is . . . a question about whether a post-Philosophical culture is a good thing to try for" (*Consequences of Pragmatism (Essays: 1972–1980)* [Minneapolis, 1982], p. xliii). And Hirsch, denying that any "decisive ground could be put forward" on behalf of either his own "realism" or what he takes to be the "idealism" of "Foucault, Heidegger, Rorty, Derrida," maintains that the

debate between these positions is, in the end, "a political, not an epistemological, issue. . . . What sort of culture do we want to foster?" ("The Politics of Theories of Interpretation," in *The Politics of Interpretation*, ed. W. J. T. Mitchell [Chicago, 1983], pp. 329, 330). For Hirsch and Rorty both, political and ethical choices replace beliefs about what is true. But how can we have any idea of what sort of culture we want to try for without already having a great many beliefs about what is true? Indeed, isn't any claim to know what culture is worth trying for already a claim to know what is true?

5. At one point in "Consequences," Stanley Fish identifies pragmatist "antifounda-tionalism" with what we have called "negative theory" (see Fish, p. 112). He goes on to observe that some writers "who profess" "antifoundationalism" nevertheless remain committed to their "own version of 'theory hope'": the hope that antifoundationalism will free us "from the hold of unwarranted absolutes so that we may more flexibly pursue the goals of human flourishing or liberal conversation" (Fish, pp. 114, 112, 113). In our view, antifoundationalists who maintain this version of theory hope are not really antifounda-tionalists at all; hence we would differ from Fish in insisting on a sharp distinction between antifoundationalism and negative theory. It is in the latter category that Rorty's position clearly belongs.